Afire With Love

AFIRE WITH LOVE

Meditations on Peace and Unity

Brother Roger of Taizé

CROSSROAD · NEW YORK

1982

The Crossroad Publishing Company
575 Lexington Avenue, New York, NY 10022

Printed in the United States of America

Translated by Emily Chisholm and the Taizé Community

Part One, "The Dynamic of the Provisional," originally
published in France under the title *Dynamique du provisoire*
1965, 1974 and in England as *The Power of the Provisional*
by Hodder & Stoughton Ltd., 1969. Part Two, "Violent
for Peace," originally published in France under the title
Violence des pacifiques 1968, 1974 and in England as *Violent
for Peace* by Darton, Longman & Todd Ltd., 1970. Part Three,
"The Wonder of a Love," originally published in France under
the title *Étonnement d'un amour* 1979, 1980.

Library of Congress Catalog Card Number: 81-71392
ISBN: 0-8245-0474-6

To Robert G. Muller

Contents

Preface

Every day throughout the year I am called to listen to young people, from different European countries or from other continents, who come week after week to our hill of Taizé. These constantly changing encounters are reflected in the following pages. The three books which are being published together in this volume were written at different periods.

When *Dynamic of the Provisional* was published, the Second Vatican Council had just ended. A wave of ecumenism was arousing tremendous hopes. But it could already be sensed that the wave would fall back if Christians did not manage to achieve, without delay, some measure of actual reconciliation.

Three years later *Violent for Peace* mirrored the student unrest of the 1960s. With many of the young we asked ourselves, "Between passivity and destructive violence, does not the Gospel suggest a third way?" And could not that third way be summed up in a seeming contradiction—the violence of peacemakers? Does not Christ say both "Happy are the peacemakers" and "Only the violent take hold the realities of the Kingdom, not those who are cold or lukewarm"?

The Wonder of a Love is a recent book. It is evident that there is a growing maturity in young people today. When we offer them hospitality in Taizé now, we are able to share with them what we have always wished for most—the fullness of a prayer, the passion of the search for God, which never causes us to forget either the building up of human society or solidarity with the deprived. On the contrary, young people live this solidarity more than ever before, more concretely than in periods that were perhaps too idealistic. A few years ago they had more ideas about changing society but fewer concrete commitments; they were often not as directly involved in real-life situations.

What captivates us most in Taizé is the reconciliation of the entire human family. If many young people are interested in the reconciliation of Christians, it is because they know that Christ wants to make the unique communion which is his Church a ferment of reconciliation and friendship for the whole human community. Their passion for the reconciliation of Christians goes hand in hand with a passion for reconciliation and peace throughout the human family.

And so they ask themselves, "Why this incoherence, this inconsistency in Christians? How can Christians prepare for peace and reconciliation between peoples if they themselves are opposed and separated, not only by the old divisions of history but by brand-new ones too?"

If Christians attempt to anticipate a reconciliation, it is not in the spirit of a crusade, nor to be stronger against others. It is to be, together, a ferment of peace even in the divisions which tear apart the human family. Their reconciliation is not without an effect on world peace.

When they are reconciled, even a small number of Christians can overturn determinisms of hatred and war, and offer a new, shining, human hope to people who otherwise would be left to sink into passivity, discouragement, and meaninglessness. By their presence Christ prepares for the healing of divisions and opens for humanity a path of hope.

Filled as we are in Taizé by this passion for a reconciliation, it is not for nothing that recently, upon awakening, one of my young brothers, an Italian, wrote down these words: "God asks of us and gives to us the passion not to abandon Christ, who suffers for his Church; that is our vocation."

BROTHER ROGER OF TAIZÉ

Part One

THE
DYNAMIC
OF THE
PROVISIONAL

Things are moving faster today than ever before. Only by living the dynamic of the provisional can we discover how, time after time, to keep on gaining new momentum. This will leave us free to advance—and we are all the freer, the more faithful we are to what is essential.

Ecumenism can only make progress if its inner dynamic drives it to become more and more universal. How else could the ecumenical wave slowly but surely gain ground among Christians and, through them, reach all of humanity?

Unless they are visible in communion, can Christians go on talking about love? In the eyes of those who watch the way we live, the very credibility of the People of God is at stake.

Toward a Wider Ecumenism

Ecumenism Is Still Limited

At present, a wave of ecumenism is arousing tremendous hopes. What can be done to ensure that this wave not only does not retreat, but gains ground little by little?

It is more urgent than ever that we use all our resources to give ecumenism a new dimension.

Ecumenism is the attempt to make visible a brotherly communion among Christians and, through them, among all people.

This is an extremely delicate mission, calling upon the resources of the whole personality and for a refusal to be satisfied with only partial involvement.

Ecumenism was born in the Western world, in a small number of groups who tried to awaken the Christian conscience in the face of a situation intolerable to anyone professing love for his neighbor. Colored by its Western origins, it has remained limited instead of attaining to the universality inherent in its nature. In particular, it has not brought us much closer to Christians of the Southern hemisphere.

It came into being, moreover, in a pluralistic society where the influence of Christians, already limited, was still further diminished by their divisions.

When the incoming tide of ecumenism is channeled by Church leaders exclusively for their own purposes, it loses its power to move the younger generations, who are more and more apprehensive of anything that bears the stamp of an institution. Of course this can lead to a kind of peaceful coexistence, which in itself is a boon. But mere coexistence means coming to a standstill. Good relations, necessary as they are, are not enough.

How many Church leaders envisage only an eschatological ecumenism—for the life to come—as if visible communion were not meant to be realized on our earth. As soon as a compelling sense of urgency is lost, we prolong indefinitely a situation in which everyone is satisfied just with being listened to by the others.

Dialogue is indispensible, but it must not settle into a static benevolence between the confessions.

The tremendous hopes aroused come up against the temptation to dwell endlessly on denominational differences in all their shapes and forms. This kind of confessionalism is an attitude of self-defense. In the past it could be justified, but today those who profess it are condemned to remaining enclosed in their own shells. Besides, denominational mentalities persist even when faith has disappeared. We all know Catholics or Protestants who profess only a vague deism, but still cling to their prejudices against other Christians.

There is one force capable of making us go beyond our confessional positions. It arises when we allow ourselves to be challenged by the millions of persons who are baptised but who have no attachment to God, and by the multitudes who are totally indifferent to the faith.

Certainly it is within ourselves that all communication and dialogue find their strongest resistance. Being open to all means overcoming our self-centeredness and allowing that Other than ourselves to penetrate the depths of our personalities.

Gestures to Bring Us Out of Ourselves

In these days paths of hope are opening up. With all the prophecies of doom that we hear, it is important to remember that very often, in the most difficult periods of history, a small number of women and men throughout the world were able to turn the course of historical developments, because they hoped against all hope. What was doomed to disintegration entered instead into the current of a new dynamism.

In order for us to advance toward a communion, God has given us the means of bringing us out of ourselves. Through the momentous events of this century, we are offered a way of emerging from the process of regression, which for several centuries has been affecting Christians so deeply.

There are three gestures, in particular, which are capable of being signs of God at work, paths of communion, and ways of discovering new dimensions of ecumenism:

Avoid separating the generations;

Go to meet those who cannot believe;

Stand alongside the exploited.

Of course some decisions will always set father against son, and Christian against Christian. There will always be separations; there will always be fanatical defenders of their own selves.

But if only all those willing to participate in a common march forward would join together now! And if only Christians already together would simply refrain from passing judgment on those who travel by other roads! It is essential to credit everyone with good intentions, even those who are desparetely defending bygone attitudes.

At the Sources of the Contemplative Life

Inspired by its generosity, the younger generation is eager to go out and encounter modern life in all its diversity. To get in touch with modern man they want to free themselves from the stock phrases and the vocabulary of the past.

We are emerging from a long period in which formulations, symbols, and signs in Christian life and prayer have not been easy to understand. The desire to make a clean sweep and find other ways of drawing near to God is a healthy reaction against all mechanical repetition, lack of participation, and stereotyped expressions.

Today we are nearing a new dawn, but in its light we can perceive that relationship with God does not do away with mystery. On the contrary, there is always a line that no one can cross and beyond which the mystery remains.

When we want to make everything clear, we run the risk of understanding nothing at all, so true it is that our intelligence alone cannot grasp the mystery of God. To enter into it, nothing is more indispensable than actions, gestures, and humble signs, which express the depths of the personality, the "archetypes," as some would say today.

Fervor cannot be nourished on explanation alone. In our life of common prayer, the gestures that have received every possible explanation will, by themselves alone, still not keep us from falling into routine.

By formulating everything, we risk losing the sense of God. This creates a vacuum into which flows indifference or even rejection, since revolt is always ready to come to life in each one of us. If we lose the sense of the mystery of God, we are tempted to turn to mockery and produce a caricature. A deep-seated force within us takes over, banishing every prompting of humility and preventing us from seeing the mystery of Christ and his Body, the Christian community.

For anyone who wants to be fully present in societies that are becoming more and more secularized without losing his sense of God, two guidelines are imperative. By means of them he will enter ever more deeply into the sources of contemplative living:

Live the mystery of the People of God;

Remain in contemplative waiting.

Avoid Separating the Generations

Accept the Present

Some people were already old when they were young. Their eyes turned toward the past, recent or distant, they cannot accept the changes taking place all around them. Far from accepting, they merely put up with them; "they sneer and shake their heads."[1]

This holds true for all social groups. So many Christians pass an irrevocable judgment on the young and thus widen the gulf between the generations. But people who grow old with no ties to the rising generations condemn themselves to vegetating. Because of the enormous changes taking place today, more than any previous generation we need to have minds and hearts open to comprehend the important developments of our time.

It is more and more the case that what we learned in our youth nowhere near approaches the levels attained by present-day knowledge. But if we use our minds day by day, they will be constantly renewed and able to adapt to new situations.

With advancing age the mind is enriched, the judgment becomes more acute and the accumulation of experience and knowledge lends an irreplaceable perceptiveness to our reflection: nothing is so valuable as a long life of hard work.

The more a man is linked to eternity, the better he disposes himself to live, for he knows what he is drawing near to. Growing old then means being rejuvenated by everything that comes to us through contemporary developments.

If the older generations have no right to impose themselves to the exclusion of others, neither can the young take advantage of their age. The Christian community is not a copy of civil societies;

everybody has their contribution to make. The generation gap goes against the spirit of ecumenism, and each one of us risks losing everything by it: the young because they no longer benefit from the human and spiritual experience their elders have acquired; the not-so-young and the elderly because they are relegated to a situation where they have no life to live, and can only wait passively for their own deaths.

One of the generations today is the hinge between two worlds, one in which parental and historical influences predominate, and another which wants nothing to do with these. It is up to those who belong to this generation to refuse to be sacrificed. If instead they see the obligation to go forward as a challenge, they will find ways of linking the mentalities of the past with the thinking of tomorrow.

It takes everybody to make ecumenism a reality, for it means, quite simply, welcoming everybody. It allows what is most genuine in each one's aspirations to blossom into fulfilment. Lagging behind hinders ecumenism, which means joining together without ever breaking anything off.

A Thirst for the Real

As I write these pages day by day, my mind is constantly kept awake here at Taizé by dialogues with many very different young people. They all have one common denominator: an intense desire to enter the world of tomorrow by participating in a rebirth of the Christian community and of the formulations of the faith.

Any sectarianism leads to a reaction of withdrawal on the part of the young who, refusing all reference to a history that no longer has anything to say to the present, will tend more and more to set themselves up in autonomous groups. Unlike their elders, the younger generation will have nothing more to do with denominational self-justifications.

They will go where there is life. They have been educated in the disciplines of technology and are eager to turn ideas into realities, so they will not put up with the delaying tactics of aged institutions much longer. If we do not discover together new paths toward communion, many young Christians will continue to search elsewhere and turn to universalist ideologies or to spirituality without God.

Conscious of their own dynamism, these generations demand authenticity. They are afraid of an abstract ecumenism, which would simply be one more idea, one more ideology. They will not stand for an ecumenism that would be just a subterfuge to mask the embarrassment of division. The hour for concrete gestures has arrived.

Among the younger generations of Christians two tendencies exist, both fired by one and the same enthusiasm. Some young people, distressed by the unwieldiness of institutions, turn their distress in to aggression. They cannot see any other way out but to break the structures and destroy the old pockets of Christian institutionalism. As far as rebuilding goes, their views are sometimes only theoretical.

Other young people, taking concrete situations into account, want to introduce a new today into the community of Christians. They know that rebirth is not a game, nor does it mean calling everything into question for the sheer pleasure of getting people all stirred up—an infernal circle in which we enclose other people to satisfy our own need for change. And so they do not wish to build in the abstract, or in isolation.

It is true that the situation which must be overcome in the next decades is characterized by several centuries of marking time; at one point each of the different groups of Christians, in order to survive, had to consolidate its own traditions, even if that meant cutting themselves off from one another. Marking time hardens and leads unfailingly to disintegration: anyone who stops creating is heading for self-destruction, in the short term or in the long.

The Gospel in its Original Freshness

The younger generation is asking for new signs. Does the Holy Spirit only speak through mature men, the wise men that we have perhaps become? Might he not also speak to the People of God through the new generations? Will their questions succeed in touching us to the quick?

At times the young judge Church leaders harshly. They feel that adults have acquired unjustifiable securities, the privileges that go with institutions, and so they refuse to enter into communication with them.

They want the Christian community to be uncompromising. They are revolted by cleverness. They demand a new life-style and, if they do not find it, they prefer to leave the Church and go where they think they see more simplicity and more sincerity in human relationships.

What is the best that this generation has to say to us? "Give us existential proof that you believe in God, and that your security is truly in Him. Prove to us that you are living the Gospel in all its original freshness, in a spirit of poverty, in solidarity with all and not only with the family of your particular Church."

The Gospel in all its freshness? That means a constantly renewed waiting for God. It means living in the dynamism of the present, continually returning to the sources. It means reconciliation.

In order to recover the original freshness of the Gospel, could we accept a second conversion? The word is inapt, charged with the emotional overtones our forebears sometimes gave it. But we adults, are we afraid of renewals that are all the more difficult because habits formed over the years and human pride run contrary to the spirit of poverty and to authentic waiting? Pride creates a cleavage through which all the freshness of the Gospel trickles away. But if we accept this conversion in its totality, Christ will enter into the depths of our minds and our hearts. He will even penetrate our bodies, so that in our turn we will have "bowels of mercy."

Creating Together

Whether they are Catholics or Protestants, the rising generations demand more than reforms: they demand a rebirth of the Christian community. But very often they put the cart before the horse, forgetting that there is no reform of community without reform of the individual. Being must come before doing. Obsessed by the will for reform, we run the risk of forgetting that renewal begins in the depths of ourselves.

To these young people I keep on saying: in the brotherly communion which brings together several generations today in Taizé, we want to listen to the Holy Spirit in you, enlarging our minds, our spirits, and our hearts. Ask God for our conversion and we will build together, and together we will say: "Look, Lord, upon your people; consider our brothers and sisters the world over. We have separated; we do not seem to be able to join together in a common creation. Break down our self-sufficiency. Inflame us all with the fire of your love."

And I also say to them: nobody constructs starting from nothing. The power of the forces that inhabit you can lead you to believe that you are going to rebuild entirely on your own. But the genius of the People of God is to construct with everybody. Do not forget yesterday. Nothing enduring is accomplished unless it is created along with others.

In the common life of the People of God as in every Christian community, including marriage, each individual member plays his part day by day in recreating the whole body. If one member is dominated by a personal creative passion, and does his work without integrating it into the creative work of the community, he destroys without realizing it.

For people really to live a common life, the aim of all must be to build together. The sign of communion that will then shine out among men is more important than the noblest piece of individual effort, worked out on the fringe of the community.

Our creative work becomes communal as soon as we consider

what God is preparing for us. So many signs are given us today. God is preparing for us a Christian community that will be a place of communion, offering to the insecure throughout the world a firm base. No violence will be used to achieve this communion. No one will ever be required to renounce his own Church or his own family. That would not be creating together. To do so would be to wound love, and anyone who wounds love is not building up the People of God.

Go to Meet Those
Who Cannot Believe

Ecumenism: The First Step

Now, at the end of the twentieth century, we Christians are confronted with the result of out divisions—mutual impoverishment.

We are surrounded by non-Christians, and also by Christians for whom the faith is a matter of indifference. They can only believe what they see with their eyes. How can they take us seriously as long as our brotherly love is not plain for all to see?

A time of confrontation is coming. We are all concerned because we are all challenged. After twenty centuries of Christianity, more and more baptized persons are losing interest in the faith. At the same time, in spite of our Christian presence throughout the world, living conditions are deteriorating year by year in certain regions of the globe.

Our communion is a function of all these people; it is for them all. We do not desire it for our own happiness, nor to be stronger over against others. We desire it solely in order to follow our vocation to be universal. That is the aim of ecumenism; it is the first step, to make us able to offer people a place of communion for all. Is not the People of God still the only reality capable of offering a brotherly communion to people all over the world?

We will never encounter those who do not believe unless we are all together. Not that we are asked to betray the truth! But if we agree on one basic truth, the necessity of visible communion, we will have found the existential possibility of agreeing one day on other truths of the faith.

There is the promise of a new dynamism to those who come togeth-er again after separation. Anyone who has achieved reconciliation finds that his mind and heart have been opened, and even in old age he renews his youth. Reconciled with himself and his neighbor, he regains vital energy. In the same way, Christians throughout the world will experience in the rediscovery of visible communion the youthfulness and vitality of a new springtime.

There is a dynamic of reconciliation that will bring us out of the state of impoverishment brought about by our divisions. Its impetus will allow us to overcome our inability to join a world which, though it may not expect much from us, would be justified in expecting everything from men and women who call themselves Christians.

But the confrontation now in preparation will mean, in the strongest sense of the word, an awakening for everyone. For all of us, together, to go and meet those who cannot believe, we are asked to make the secret offering of our lives day by day.

The real history of the ecumenical movement will never be writ-ten. It lies in the faithfulness in things large and small of those whose whole inner life is engaged in the stuggle. For a long time to come ecumenism will be advancing against the stream of confor-mity; dialogue with those farthest from us will never happen as a matter of course. Anyone who is unwilling to accept this struggle should ask himself if his ecumenism is not a plant without roots.

Dialogue with Everyone

At Taizé the vocation to ecumenism has made us open, year in year out, to all that is human. It has awakened in us an interest in those who were farthest from us. Without a passion for the unity of the Body of Christ, we never would have discovered this friendship with so many people all over the world.

Our concern for dialogue has made us attentive to everything human. Who would not burn with desire to understand another human being in his life struggle: the light that has gone from his eyes or the hard-won serenity, the whole personality held in check, the scars of conflicting impulses, the generous gift of himself or the firm will to keep himself back.

The spirit of mercy disposes the heart of stone to become a heart of flesh. It leads to a strong love, devoid of sentimentality, that caricature of tenderness. It refuses to turn the spotlight on oneself. It invites us to accept in quiet trust our neighbor, whoever he may be, and any event whatsoever.

Why is it that, although they say they know God, so many Christians behave as if they had never found him? They show no mercy. They profess the God of Jesus Christ and yet their hearts remain hard.

On the other hand, why is it that so many agnostics, in the wake of the publicans and tax-collectors, "are entering the Kingdom ahead of us"? They open up a way of peace, they are men and women of communion, and they often show greater concern for peacemaking than many Christians do.

It is possible to believe that people of this kind are unconsciously bearers of Christ, although they have no explicit faith. Could this not be the result of the prayers of so many Christians throughout the ages? People hear God's voice without recognizing him; they are obedient to him and they live lives of charity. How can we avoid applying the words of Christ to them: "They go before us into the Kingdom?"[2] They open doors for us; they clear the way.

There are many who profess to love Christ but do not know him. And there are many who love him, although they claim that they do not know him.

There are many who are children of light unawares. In any case they are easy to recognize: full of concern for their neighbors, they flee the works of darkness, all that is murky and lacking in transparence.

Dialogue with someone who does not believe sometimes allows us to discover in him what he does not recognize by himself, the mystery of a hidden presence.

A Christian who senses in his neighbor the most ecumenical qualities, who seeks in him the being God created, benefits from the mutual recreation involved in all dialogue.

Only someone whose life is animated at all times by the Word of God and the Eucharist can speak like this, of course. Otherwise the result would be relativism, which does nobody any good. To say that there are people who follow God without knowing him could constitute an invitation to cease all combat for Christ. What then would be the good of praying, or of remaining in God's presence?

Stand Alongside the Exploited

The Clash Between Two Worlds

Christians are becoming more and more aware of the conditions of injustice and oppression that characterize human relationships. This realization needs to be continually brought up to date. On re-reading this chapter after nine years with a view to a new edition, I now find that what I wrote then did not go far enough. And so I have retained only a few passages.

One day an intolerable divorce will cleave the world in two, if those who live in the Northern hemisphere remain indifferent to the two thousand million whose poverty continues to increase, in the Southern hemisphere as well as in vast areas of the rich countries. If, together with them, we do not seek to advance toward the liberation of mankind from oppression of every sort, the meeting of two worlds could well turn into an ever widening rift.

An economic and cultural system worked out in the Northern hemisphere has brought the Southern continents to the state of dependency with which we are familiar. The continents of the North are met more and more by curt refusals from the Southern hemisphere. And in the Northern hemisphere many are beginning to consider their own privileges intolerable.

If only Christians were able to make Peter's words come true: "I have neither gold nor silver,"[3] I have no capital in reserve and nothing superfluous, the course of many an historical evolution would be turned back. The struggle to set every human being free, the struggle to promote a society without classes would find a base of support. The rising generations desert us Christians who speak glibly of security in God when we often need so much insurance in gold and silver.

But today, still more is required of us. Generosity and detachment are not enough. Communion with the poverty-stricken in the world also means participating in the world's struggle against its poverty. The Christians' place is in the thick of this struggle, at the front lines, in the rich countries as well as in the poor.

The Spirit of Poverty

Today a strong call for poverty is making itself heard among Christians. Many young people are critical of every sign of wealth. Throughout history, to this very day, so much wealth has been accumulated by Christians, and by the Churches themselves. Christians have moved further and further away from the "socialization" that was a fact in the early Church.

Poverty is a word that scorches the lips. When I was writing the Rule of Taizé, I hardly dared use it; my pen could scarcely bring itself to write it. Thinking that the spirit of poverty lay first and foremost in simple sharing, I preferred to speak of a commitment to community of goods "that might imply possible poverty."

We may have to give up many material possessions, but the spirit of poverty goes still further. Poverty of means might lead us to seek compensations elsewhere, for example by commandeering other people, forcing them to fit into our scheme of things.

The spirit of poverty embraces the whole of our being. External signs of poverty are not enough. They do not prevent us from still cherishing a human ambition, a need for power or a desire to dominate sometimes belied by outward appearances.

Sometimes too a puritanical attitude prevails. It consists in acting poor, in other words looking drab, when wealth is hiding behind the faded exterior. "Happy the heart that is poor." If the spirit of poverty became synonymous with gloom and austerity, how would it correspond to the first Beatitude? The spirit of poverty is found in the joy of a man who trusts in God. It shows itself in outward signs of joy.

There are also those who advocated an ideal of poverty unattainable in an affluent society. They place those who want to be poor according to the Gospel in a state of pemanent conflict: they desire to attain the inaccessible. To ask for the impossible leads to crisis situations. Insisting too much can imprison a man in his inner conflicts. Are we not witnessing, in some circles, the establishment of a neo-Jansenism?

It is true that many men and women have taken a vow of poverty in response to a radical call. When their poverty is lived without passing judgment on others, it is joyful waiting for Christ to return, and genuine solidarity with those throughout the world who have no daily bread. It is, as well, the protest of the Christian conscience at the abuse of the earth's riches and at exploitation. The earth has been given to man for his use. It is a means of liberation, not of impairing the freedom of others.

If it is accompanied by fanaticism, a commitment to poverty is not only unedifying—the bitterness it contains is destructive. The man or woman who has taken a vow of poverty must not forget the father or mother of a family whose way of life is very different. People who are fanatically poor are frightening.

The spirit of poverty does not lead to complacency. One Beatitude cannot be exaggerated at the expense of the others. The poor are gentle; they remain Christ's poor. Without charity poverty is nothing—shadow without light.

Within the poeple of Israel there was a community of poor people. They lived in the presence of God, awaiting the coming of the Messiah, eager for the imminent fulfilment of the promise. The accumulation of possessions would have given the lie to their hope. In this community the Virgin Mary was ready and willing, and she was able to pronounce the yes of a faithful heart.

Today among suffering humanity throughout the world, many belong to the community of Christ's poor. Some more than others, they are eagerly living and waiting for his return. Among them can be found one of the great treasures of the Gospel, which Western

Christians, enervated by the accelerating pace of developments, are losing: the awareness of God's providence. As we take part in their struggle, we do indeed discover a sense of urgency, but at the same time we learn that waiting can be dynamic. Through them we become capable of understanding what our dense minds could no longer comprehend.

Inspired by the spirit of poverty, a man learns to depend on God. We are poor in skills, poor in resources; but he is there, and he fills us to overflowing. Multiplying securities of all kinds gives the lie to our trust in God. Abandoning them means seeking God and finding unshakeable security in him alone. In the wilderness the people of Israel tried to keep the manna from heaven for the morrow, but it was already going bad.

Living the Mystery
of the People of God

Solidarity With All the Baptized

The ecumenical vocation leads us inevitably to reflect upon the People of God and in particular to realize that by their baptism all Christians belong to Christ and to his Body. Orthodox, Catholic, Protestant, we are all stamped with the seal of the universal by one and the same baptism, and intended to become people able to discern in every creature the image of the Creator himself.

We all confess in the same way our relationship to Christ, the Head, and to his Body, the People of God. When we declare "I believe in . . . the communion of saints," we are affirming: I believe that between the witnesses who have left us and the Christians on earth who struggle and pray, there exists a relationship that nothing can destroy. An identical communion binds together all the baptized who are alive on earth today. Because of this common baptism by which we are all rooted in Christ, we are asked to live in solidarity with all the baptized and to remain in unshakeable fellowship.

For a Catholic, to be in solidarity with all the baptized means first of all being in solidarity with all the spiritual families, which are the soul of Catholicism. At this stage of history, we expect Catholics not to reject one another. If the various tendencies that are manifest were to prevent dialogue, it would be an unparalleled setback for ecumenism.

In the midst of their disarray, may those who have a sense of the things that endure, a sense of the holy, see in the Christians opposite them men and women with an overriding conern for dialogue with those who are far from the faith. May those who have been granted a sense of the mystery of the Church refrain from keeping for themselves the irreplaceable values to which they are attached, and understand those who have a passion for dialogue with their contemporaries. And may the Catholics who are in the front lines learn once again that, without a daily return to the sources, very soon they will have nothing to offer but their own emptiness.

After an initial period of inevitable tension, we hope all the various spiritual families will discover the Gospel values each of them contains.

A Christian's life is demanding enough as it is! Why waste energy in condemning? Why wear ourselves out in despising other schools of thought? Any argument arising from blind hatred proves nothing.

How many Christians are still capable of wielding anathemas, particularly in minority situations of whatever denominational background, as if constant defensiveness were their only means of survival! In their aggressiveness such people always claim that another school of thought is not representative. But what are the people who speak like this representing? What light are they shedding in the world of today and among the People of God in its march forward?

We are very often particularly hypersensitive in what concerns our own confessional positions. Did not our fathers risk their lives to defend these very positions? Dwelling on the past history of battles and of tears paralyzes our energies. Our sensitivity quickly overflows and becomes exaggerated, and then, to avoid being bruised, retreats into its shell. A refusal to brood over yesterday's wounds and today's is the only way out.

Nothing is more contrary to solidarity than a double-faced ecumenism, and ecumenism with no risks attached. Those practicing it show much kindness and balanced judgment in their dialogue with Christians of another persuasion, but they criticize the others as soon as they are safely back in their own camp. In so doing they gain credit with those who are in favor of ecumenism, as long as everything stays just as it has always been.

This equivocal attitude, not to say this ecumenical "double life," is one of the supreme temptations. It is the prelude to future disappointments. To call oneself ecumenical, and all the time be afraid of unity, leads to impounding the ecumenical wave in the institution, stopping it from rebounding and causing it to fall back again.

Toward, Not Away

In 1519, as he was commenting on the Biblical text "help carry one another's burdens, and so you will fulfil the law of Christ,"[4] Luther seized the opportunity to say what he thought about the schism of the Hussites in Bohemia, which had taken place before the Reformation:

> The Bohemians who have separated from the Roman Church can indeed bring forward excuses for what they did, but these excuses are blasphemous and contrary to all Christ's commands. Their separation is in fact contrary to the love which sums up all the commandments. What they advance as their only argument is precisely the worst accusation against them: they claim that they have separated for fear of the Lord and on grounds of conscience, in order not to live among corrupt priests and popes. Even if priests or popes or anybody else were corrupt, if you were burning with true Christian love, you would not run away, you would go running towards them, from the ends of the earth if need be, to weep, to exhort, to persuade and to set everything going again.
>
> Know that in obedience to this teaching of the apostle ("carry one another's burdens"), what you must carry are not the pleasant things, but the burdens; which means that all the glory of those Bohemian brethren is nothing but outward show. It is the light in which the angel of Satan is disguised.
>
> And we, are we going to run away and separate because we have to bear the burdens and the truly intolerable monsters of the Court of Rome? Far from it! Far from it! On the contrary, we reprimand, we are incensed, we plead, we exhort, but we do not break the unity of the Spirit, and we do not stand on our dignity. For we know that

love overcomes all things, not only defective institutions, but also
men who are monsters of iniquity. A love which bears only the good
qualities of another is a lie.[5]

Luther took the initiative that was to lead to division in the sixteenth century. Yet he had an acute sense of the Church, otherwise
no such passage could ever have come from his pen. He was not
aware of any definitive break, still less of the consequences we perceive today. What he went through, along with many others of his
time, was a dilemma of conscience. Perhaps we would not be
where we are today if the confrontation made possible by the Second Vatican Council had taken place in the sixteenth century. How
many times during Council sessions did I call to mind the figure of
Martin Luther! I used to say to myself: if that man were here in St.
Peter's, he could only rejoice at hearing his most fundamental
aims expressed in this place, the aspirations which, initially, were
closest to his heart and inspired his actions. But the clock of
history cannot be turned back.

Neither was generosity lacking on the Catholic side in the sixteenth
century. Some expressed genuine distress and worry. In 1522, the
Diet of Nuremberg called the German princes together to decide
on a common policy toward Luther and the dawning Reformation.
Pope Adrian VI sent a legate to whom he had given these written
instructions:

> You must say that we freely acknowledge that God has permitted
> this persecution because of the sins of men, priests and prelates in
> particular. Holy Scripture teaches us throughout that the faults of
> the people most often have their source in the faults of the clergy.
> That is why, when our Lord wanted to purify the unhealthy city of
> Jerusalem, he first went into the temple to pray. We know that for
> years now, even in the Holy See, many abominations have been
> committed: the abuse of holy things, transgression of the command-
> ments, so much so that everything has been turned into scandal. All
> of us, prelates and clergy have forsaken the way of righteousness.[6]

In one sense, the vocation of the Reformation was initially the determination to amend and deepen Catholicism. Protestantism, however, has sometimes set itself up in an isolation untrue to its original insights. The danger, then, is that this can lead to an attitude of simply waiting for the Catholic Church to "become Protestant."

In the long run positions hardened. What was a dilemma of conscience was superseded by attitudes of defensiveness or complacency on both sides. Those who did not ask for the break made the most of their being in the right, and those who brought it about believed they were on the right side of the fence—hadn't they weeded out the tares from the wheat?

Catholics and Protestants formed defensive blocs. To protect her members and to preserve them from new separations, the Catholic Church set in motion and encouraged a movement of Counter-Reformation. In many respects her thinking developed in opposition to Protestantism. On the Protestant side, confessional systems of thought were based on the negation of anything that appeared to be Catholic. Furthermore, in the course of its history Protestantism has included minorities which have had to justify their existence over against a Catholic majority. This formed habits of defensiveness so characteristic of a certain mentality.

If both sides do all they can to promote the rebirths that are essential, the day will dawn when we realize that have come together again. If renewal is put into practice by both parties, they will meet at the end of the road. The insights born of the Reformation as well as those of the Catholic tradition will be seen to complement each other and will be brought into harmony.

The most successful renewals will no doubt always leave lingering elements of sectarianism in their wake. But that should not make us lose heart.

On the Catholic side, the Second Vatican Council has opened a way forward, a way full of promise and dynamism. An event of God has burst forth, at the risk of terrifying some non-Catholics who are afraid of being engulfed in a tidal wave. But once the initial shock is over, the most alert of the non-Catholics will have taken stock of this event.

It is up to Protestants to make up their minds whether, for their part, they are going to keep on looking back to their past history or whether they, in their turn, will accept the possiblity of rebirth.

After four and a half centuries we are forced to admit that a renewal in Protestantism is necessary for it to rediscover that dynamic of the provisional, which should have been the reason for its existence—not to settle down so as to last forever. It is true that this renewal is not made any easier when some Catholics speak of the "return" of their separated brethren. This expression hurts, because it suggests a retrograde movement, an unconditional surrender. Such a conception is far from the mentality of contemporary man, who tends always to move forward and to leap over obstacles. Communion among Christians will not be the triumph of some over others. If it had to be victory for some and defeat for others, nobody would accept it.

Protestants today are in danger of living under two illusions.

As heirs of a Reformation, they could think that the reforms have been made once and for all. They believed they had rediscovered the purity characteristic of the Church in its first flowering. But it is difficult for them to agree even on a common conception of the early Church, and on the point in time when this first period ended. Have not their own communities, moreover, been infected by complacency, and by the accumulation of traditions, institutions, and doctrinal developments further and further removed from the original thinking of the Reformation? Their institutions are weighed down with more than four centuries of history. Who will be able to promote a new and profound rebirth, so that they can speak to contemporary man?

Another illusion would be to assume that, as a result of the reforms issuing from the Second Vatican Council, Catholicism is going to "protestantize" itself. Would that not be fostering a "return to the fold" mentality in no way different from that for which Protestants reproach others? As if they only had to remain as they are, and wait for the Catholics to come to them. "God's good time" is here today. Will they be able to welcome it in simplicity of heart and humility? Are they going to retreat into new self-justifications, or will they be able to do everything possible to exhort, persuade, support, and bring to fulfillment rebirths of the People of God?

It may be necessary to react to the dead weight of a Christian community. But if those who express themselves in this way become protesters and if, moreover, they regroup and clamor from without, they hold back the Christian community, exhausted as it is from its long journey, and they hinder its rebirth. How can we become leaven in the dough, to raise it up and to burst the crust which continually reforms over aging institutions? Nothing can resist such leaven.

Threatening to break off relations is a dangerous tactic. It is always from within and with infinite patience that what should be revived is revived. And it is only then that confrontation becomes creative. Though at the time it seems to ease tension, every break is an impoverishment in the long run. It is a refusal to move ahead and to undertake the ventures essential to every life in God that is fully responsible and in solidarity with one's neighbors.

The temptation is indeed great for some to pull back and then, with the best people, form a little Church group. But we must realize that under the pressures of history, "tiny remnants" run the risk of fossilizing and of no longer being bearers of life. And all that does not promote life is doomed to die.

The diversity of spiritual families within the People of God makes for health and universality. But those whose particularities can only subsist at the price of separation militate against unity.

Reflecting on the mystery of the People of God, accepting our own impotence in the face of certain encumbrances, enables us at the right time to ask, to plead, to exhort, and to prepare for the explosion of God's event in the midst of the Christian community, but without ever breaking the communion.

Anyone who, in his personal or his Church life, is content simply to wait for God to act and to live solely in the provisional, will soon see his waiting invalidated. If he refuses to accept that the event of God must enter into history and into the continuity of tradition, he will expose it to the danger of being like a pearl cast before swine.

But on the other hand, anyone who does not allow for the constant possibility of the event of God forgets the value of waiting, deprives himself of the dynamic of the provisional and condemns himself to fossilization and the darkening of his light. To maintain stereotyped forms in the name of tradition is to caricature the tradition itself, that great stream flowing through the ages and the life of the People of God, bearing in it and with it essential values, the living Word of God. Anyone who expects nothing new becomes static. He loses all ability to communicate.

It can happen that when God acts decisively in the Christian community there is great tension, great suffering even. Then, more than ever, contemplation of Christ and attentiveness to the mystery of the People of God come to the aid of our impatience and bring us serenity once more.

Healing the Break

The call for reconciliation and solidarity is a language meaningful to everybody. Too often those in authority are tempted to label naive the faith of men and women who, to prove that things are on the move, forge ahead and act in ways which go against the stream. It is a serious matter to caricature the way in which the humble express their faith, and to mistake a childlike spirit for childishness. To call naive or sentimental the assurance of those who, in the simplicity of their prayer, count on God for everything, is to cast doubts on the seriousness of their faith.

Here are two couples, both separated but desiring reconcilation. The first looks backward and does not live in God's today. Both partners want to justify themselves, to have guarantees, to teach the other a lesson. Good reasons pile up over and over again; arguments multiply. Encounter remains impossible.

The second couple has a kind of presentiment: if the family is to exist again one day, the time comes when there is no other solution but to come together under the same roof and try to live and get along together. This means they have to refuse to accuse one another, to give up once and for all their belief that separation is justified, and discover themselves and each other in a brand-new solidarity. Once the introductory dialogue is over, communion between Christians will not be accomplished without the act of faith, which consists in making our solidarity visible, by living together in the same Church reality. Those who are separated and eagerly await communion realize that their situation is provisional, and this stimulates them to advance. For those who refuse to give up hope, the price to be paid for communion between Christians is this: at all times they must be able to keep going forward beyond their own limitations, in the most ecumenical setting possible.

The Eucharist, which is at one and the same time the source and the goal of unity, is alone capable of giving us the strength and the means of making communion among Christians a reality on this earth. This is a vital truth. The sacrament of communion is offered to us to dissolve all the ferments of separation in and around us. By it those who despise one another through ignorance are bound together.

The ecumenical wave will fall back if the day does not soon arrive when those members of different Churches who believe in the real presence of Christ in the Eucharist all meet around the same Table.

Servants of Unanimity

The ministry of authority in the People of God is often called into question. These doubts correspond to a mentality that rejects anything that stems from the previous generations.

This ministry in the People of God exists for the sole purpose of fostering communion. It is there to gather together, to unite those who are always separating, dividing, and opposing. Those who have received this function are above all servants. Their pastoral task, their service, is to help the Christian community entrusted to them to move toward unanimity, that is to say, literally, to have only one soul, *una anima*.

Every Christian community is a microcosm, a visible image of communion. It cannot exist without a head, someone who has received the office of uniting, if need be exhorting, and above all of reminding everyone of the spirit of mercy without which no Christian community is possible. If the Church requires, at the head of each community, someone who fosters unanimity, who regroups what always tends to disperse, should she not also accept a pastor of pastors and communities who will be tireless in keeping them all together?

And yet many refuse these ministries of communion, asserting that Church leaders, more than other men, give in to ambition. It is true that pride and vanity are pitfalls lying in wait for those holding positions of authority in the Church.

Human ambition is utterly opposed to poverty of spirit. When it slowly gains ground, it must always find new pastures. Developments in contemporary psychology often create a will to "self-fulfilment." How many have run after that mirage, the ambition to "fulfil themselves"! But what does this expression mean in terms of the Gospel?

One of the great combats to be waged against oneself is indeed the struggle for humility, and it is a virtue sorely put to the test in anyone who accepts responsibility. The slaking of pride brings temporary relief, but the craving for power returns, more and more insatiably.

Those who hold such positions in the heart of Christian communities sometimes yield to the same inner tendencies—authoritarianism, intrigue, and seeking relief from humiliating wounds in the compensations of ambition. Nonhierarchical institutions do not protect those in charge and do not place them in a privileged position. Protestant pastors too have been known to become victims of an inhuman religious establishment. Authoritarianism creeps in everywhere, among the leaders of Protestant Churches as well. Do not some of them have precisely that thirst for power that they sometimes criticize in those belonging to a hierarchical Church?

Nowadays men entrusted with responsibilities are sometimes unable to find time for converse with God. In many cases men overburdened with duties come to give first priority to coping with their overwhelming tasks. For lack of time, they sometimes give up their dialogue with God. Their innumerable activities no longer permit them to find in God the necessary perspective on things.

An understanding of these human situations allows us to live something of the mystery of the People of God.

Inserted into History

In creating a common life at Taizé, our sole desire was to be a family of brothers committed to following Christ, as an existential sign of the communion of the People of God.

A life in community is a living microcosm of the Church, an image on a small scale containing the whole reality of the People of God. And so the humble sign of a community can find a resonance far beyond the limitations of the individuals who make it up.

The world of today needs images more than ideas. No idea can be accepted unless it is clothed in visible reality, otherwise it is only ideology. However weak the sign, it takes on its full value when it is a living reality.

To live out our ecumenical vocation authentically, we must be deeply concerned to realize a communion in our life together. The fact that some of us belong to different Reformation Churches or to the Anglican Communion, and that it is possible to have Catholic brothers as well, does not in any way put up barriers between us. The communion of faith is forged through liturgical prayer, and takes shape slowly.

We know that we are not in a privileged situation, for our combat is intense. But if we had to start all over again, we would not hesitate.

With the great freedom given by our situation, we might well have taken no account of those who preceded us in the common life. But what sort of a life would that have been, lived outside of all solidarity? Being attentive to the mystery of the People of God has led us to consider that Taizé is only a simple bud grafted on a great tree, without which it could not survive.

In this regard it is undoubtedly significant that our village lies between Cluny and Citeaux.

On the one hand Cluny, the great Benedictine tradition that humanized everything it touched. Cluny, with its sense of moderation, of visible community built up in unity. Cluny, the center of attraction for men consciously or unconsciously seeking their own inner unity and unity with their neighbors.

Among the abbots of Cluny is the figure of that outstanding Christian, Peter the Venerable, so human, so concerned for charity and for unity, capable of gestures centuries ahead of his time. So it was that when two popes had been elected by the conclave, he was magnanimous enough to ask the one who belonged to Cluny, one of his own brothers, to step down for the sake of unity.

In advance of the thinking of his time, he welcomed and offered shelter to Abelard, a man public opinion had condemned.

At that period of history it was he, once more, who inspired his contemporaries by announcing in words of fire the power of a personal encounter:

> Jesus will always be with me, and he will never turn away from me at any time. Certainly not at any time, for, despising and rejecting all

that is not he, I will attach myself to him alone. Jesus will be my life, my food, my rest, my joy. He will be for me my country and my glory. Jesus will be everything for me: here below as far as possible, in home and love until the gate of eternity: then I shall see him face to face. He has promised.[7]

On the other hand there is Citeaux, revitalized in Peter the Venerable's time by another Christian no less remarkable: Saint Bernard.

Saint Bernard foreshadows all the reforming zeal that was to explode in the sixteenth century. He renewed Citeaux to reform the Rule by which Cluny lived. He refused to compromise the absolute of the Gospel in any way. He spoke the language of a Reformer. He was more concerned with the demands of the present moment than with historical continuity. To one of his brothers he wrote:

There is nothing stable in this world . . . and so, of necessity, we must either go forward or go back. To remain in the state one has reached is impossible. Anyone unwilling to advance retreats. It is Jesus Christ who is the prize of the race. If you stop when he is striding on, you not only come no closer to the goal, but the goal itself retreats from you.[8]

Fusing the sense of urgency with a sense of the continuity assured by several generations is an incomparable factor making for inner peace and humility: I am a useless servant; what I do not accomplish myself, others will accomplish after me. From what is now still immature, others will be able to gather the ripe fruit.

We are grateful to those who have gone before us for remaining consistently faithful to the call of the Gospel. We were all called to one and the same commitment to leave all, and to receive a hundredfold here on earth, together with persecutions.

By witness of their life as brothers, which has so often evoked the comment: "See how they love one another," by their obedience to God manifested in the humble fidelities of everyday life, by the continuity of their praise throughout the centuries, by many other qualities of life kept alive down the ages, they support us and give us grounds for hope. In some periods of history they have maintained through a great diversity of spiritual families the unity necessary for the building up of the Body of Christ. By being living signs of communion in this way, and by offering their lives day after day anew, they lead us onward in the very footsteps of Christ.

If we are told about the difficulties that weigh upon some of them, we keep silent. It is so true that judgments from outside have always led to a hardening of positions. When some of them suffer, our only wish is to love them all the more. And should the opportunity arise of expressing our own view, we do so only when we are sure of not fostering a spirit of antagonism. Otherwise we would be giving the lie to our ecumenical vocation. We would be protesters, and in that way imprison ourselves in a positon of self-sufficiency. Implicit in our very existence would be a judgment no less severe for being unexpressed. Communion cannot come about through protest. Our readiness to stigmatize another's faults from without can only shut him up in himself.

At this turning point in contemporary history, it becomes more urgent than ever before for us all to consider the essence of our common life, and to make the adaptations that need to be made. By its very nature every community life is turned toward both God and men. If it encouraged purity of life alone, it would be in danger of dying a slow death. It calls for the capacity to adapt to renewals. Those living in community use the freedom of their situation to best advantage when they are an hour ahead by the clock of human societies and that of the Church. Being too far ahead would do nobody any good. But lagging behind would destroy the momentum of a life given for others.

Today more than ever, when it is charged with the life-force proper to it, when it is filled with the freshness of brotherly love which is its distinctive feature, community life is like yeast at work in the dough. It can raise mountains of apathy, and bring to men an irreplaceable quality of the presence of Christ.

Remaining in Contemplative Waiting Upon God

Waiting and the Provisional

How often, when we are together in church for common prayer, I am in a state of amazement! These men, my brothers, my lifelong companions, remain faithful in their contemplative waiting upon God. They wait in God's presence without seeing, without knowing what the response to their waiting will be. I marvel at the earnestness of these men, their faithfulness, and the joy that dominates their inner combat.

It is so true that during our whole lives as Christians we are always in a state of waiting. Since Abraham, the first believer, and with all who come after him, we are waiting for God, for his justice, and for the event that will come from him. For anyone who has stopped waiting, anyone who has settled down in himself, his privileges, or his rights, a whole dimension of faith has shrivelled away.

To realize this means realizing as well that we are living in a state that is always provisional. Provisional has the same root as provide. Provide the measures necessary until another set of circumstances arises.

At Taizé, we are convinced that all that constitutes our particular family spirit, for example our Rule and our liturgical prayer, will perhaps disappear one day. Our liturgy, that powerful means of molding us into one communion of faith, and our Rule are instruments which make it possible for us to live in the hope of unity. In some respects are they not simply provisional elements, bound to disappear the day when all Christians are once again visibly in communion?

Anyone who lives in the provisional sees his progress constantly reinvigorated, for the supreme danger would be to become self-sufficient, to fasten the strap round our treasure trove, a liturgy for instance, and thus set up for centuries to come structures which would very quickly turn into factors producing isolation.

Can we not see in Christian history so many institutions which, in an endeavor to endure through the ages, have lost the provisional character of their beginnings? The Christian vision of their adherents becomes narrower and narrower. They can only survive by digging in behind protective barriers.

There is no reconciliation without mutual sacrifices. On the day when visible communion between Christians becomes a reality, we will have to die to ourselves, and sometimes die to what was most characteristic of the family we used to live with at a certain time and place.

What will have to disappear are the characteristics peculiar to the family, and certainly not the elements common to all. For Christian couples as for ourselves, the basis of our vocation is unalterable, particularly the vows and promises. These cannot be called into question because they constitute not only the way in which we commit ourselves to follow Christ, but the framework that keeps us together as one family.

It must be said that only someone with a sense of continuity can benefit from the dynamic of the provisional. Enthusiasm, fervor, is a positive force, but it is by no means enough. It burns itself out and vanishes if it does not transmit its momentum to another force, deeper and less perceptible, which enables us to keep on going our whole life long. It is indispensable to ensure continuity, for times of enthusiasm alternate with periods of lifelessness, arid deserts.

So it is with regularity in prayer. To complain about the faithfulness necessary would be, in fact, to complain about oneself; one day, the regularity and the continuity will be the springboard for a new leap forward.

Both are needed: enthusiasm in the perspective of the provisonal, and continuity in the perspective of hope.

People of Peace

The ecumenical vocation is assuredly ordeal by fire, a combat that requires complete self-mastery. In the face of tensions, only contemplative waiting allows us to preserve that inner vitality that comes from our love for Christ and for his Body, the Church. In order not to get bogged down in useless discussions or justifications that satisfy nobody, and above all to keep alive a vision of the needs of contemporary society, it is vital for our wills to be tempered in the wellsprings of contemplation.

No one who does not quench his thirst there can remain serene in the face of attitudes that must be analyzed if they are not to bring us to a dead halt in our progress, attitudes that otherwise may well sap our vital energies.

There are the pressures to conform in various ways, and the resistances to all the changes that unity will require. There are the Church leaders who call themselves ecumenists, yet keep postponing the day of visible communion so that, in fact, they exclude its possibility. There is also the small-mindedness of people, by no means uncultured, who seem to have an irresistible need to put labels on their neighbors, twisting the meaning of their words in an attempt to stifle all dialogue. There is incomprehensible jealousy, an open sore in the People of God. Jealousy seeks compensation by neutralizing the dynamism of new ventures.

Was it not Bernanos who wrote that all adventures of the spirit are a *via crucis*?

Every road to reconciliation involves a continual dying to self. None of those who travel this road can avoid trials and sufferings, even if they are sometimes tempted to run away from them.

To every Christian community God gives a place of peace and joy where we can rest in him alone and pass through both trials and days of gladness. Conversing with God stimulates fervor. It sets us in the communion of all the saints, alive or departed. It prepares and nourishes our communication with others by making us reflect God as bearers of his peace.

When, with two of my brothers, I met Pope John XXIII for the last time, he explained to us how he came to his decisions in very simple prayer, in serenity, in conversation with God. "I have a dialogue with God," he said, adding immediately: "Oh! very humbly. Oh! quite simply."

When someone converses with God, he does not expect any extraordinary illuminations. He knows that the most important thing, for himself and for others, is peace. Anyone who listens, by day or through the long watches of the night, is given the answer: peace!

Inner peace! Not a peace uttered by the lips while within there is war. Not a peace acquired once and for all, for there is still the burden of our own self and the incompletely healed wounds in which all kinds of feelings are still festering—bitterness, the passions seething in our flesh, illusions of impossible love or the discontent of love disappointed. All this weighs us down and tears us apart, but the peace of Christ is able to reach into the depths, even into the deepest wounds of our being.

Peace is not inner passivity nor escape from our neighbor. The peace of Christ has nothing in common with that insipid tranquillity in which the horizon contracts more and more, and in the end crushes the victim it encloses.

No peace is possible if we forget our neighbor. Every day the same question rings out: "What have you done with your brother?" A peace that does not lead to communication and brotherly communion is nothing but illusion. The man who is at peace with himself is led to his neighbor. He inspires reconciliation and peace among those who are divided.

The peace of Christ needs time to mature, for it must heal the wounds of trials and sufferings. But now they no longer overflow;

they are kept within oneself, and their hidden presence releases vital energy.

By his inner harmony with God, a man of peace is already an anticipation of unity. He carries others along with him.

Bearers of Ecumenicity

At Taizé we have discovered that commitment to the chastity of celibacy is intimately linked up with contemplative waiting on God. How else could this sign of an exclusive love for God be fully authentic?

When I master my body and keep it in subjection,[9] controlling it by watching, praying, and working, it is solely for love of Jesus Christ. No other is able to sustain an undertaking of this kind.

In refusing monasticism, the Reformation undermined celibacy as well. It is surprising to discover that for centuries the entire Reformation joined in a conspiracy of silence around the Scriptural texts concerning celibacy. It was seen as justified only in exceptional cases, as a means of ensuring greater availability. But the motive force behind chastity, the expectation of Christ's return, celibacy as a sign of the coming Kingdom, all that disappeared from the thinking of the Reformation.

When Luther broke his monastic vows, not only life in community, but also the vocation and the commitment to celibacy, almost completely disappeared from Protestantism. When we want to attack a position we are tempted to caricature it: cases of immorality were generalized, and the call of the Gospel disqualified for centuries.

Today men committed in a community or in the priesthood try to discover in our life at Taizé a confirmation of their call to celibacy, since we were under no obligation to look in that direction. The basis for any solidarity that exists lies in our common endeavor to live authentically this mysterious call of Christ.

God designates ambassadors of Christ those who, despite their human limitations, respond with the yes and amen of a faithful heart.

Celibacy opens our ecumenical vision to incomparable dimensions. Through it we want to be men whose lives are so completely focused on the hope of God that they wish to keep nothing back for themselves. This involves an exercise in opennness to the universal, a truly ecumenical openness which allows us, with hearts ready and waiting, to take on all the concerns of our neighbor, all that comes our way.

To anyone who has no family of his own, God give a heart and a mind able to love every family, human or spiritual. Anyone whose arms, for Christ's sake and the Gospel's, are open to all, enclosing no one person, is able to live the demands of ecumenicity and so understand every human situation. Any seeker after God who makes Christ his first love finds it possible to assure a hidden presence of Christ among people who cannot believe.

What is expressed here represents a discovery we have made at Taizé, and might appear to exclude marriage. But it cannot be repeated too often: the vocation to celibacy can only enhance the value of the vocation to marriage. A life of fidelity to the marriage bond can likewise only be lived in waiting on God.

The community of marriage contains in miniature so many ecclesial values! Some Church fathers called it a "little Church." Those who struggle, day after day, to remain faithful in an indissoluble unity are bearers of ecumenicity in their own right.

Intimacy and Solitude

A good part of people's energy is consumed in attempting to live lives of complete emotional fulfilment. Man hungers for intimacy with other human beings. And his passionate quest drives him to desire human relationships with nothing held back, communication with no reservations. Intimacy appears to be a goal without which no earthly happiness is possible, and its image is alluring as no other.

Any self-examination leads to the conclusion that every intimate relationship, even between the most united partners, inevitably has its limitations. Beyond them, we are alone. Anyone who refuses to accept this natural order of things will, as a result of his refusal, find himself in revolt.

Accepting our fundamental aloneness sets us on the road to peace, and allows the Christian to discover a previously unknown dimension of his relationship with God. Acceptance of this portion of loneliness, a condition of every human life, fosters intimacy with Him who rescues us from the overwhelming solitude of the man alone with himself.

To say to Christ "I love you" leads us to embody our intention in a gesture or an action, if it is not to remain mere words. If we are willing, for Christ's sake, to fight out our inner combats to the very end, even though we may, for the time being, be wounded to the quick, then intimacy with Him will fill our solitudes; from then on someone will be there.

Intimacy with Him will be communion and will sustain a faith able to move mountains.

Contemplative Waiting

The contemplative life is not an existence hovering between heaven and earth, in ecstasy or illumination. It begins when in humility we come closer to God and to our neighbor. It is always stamped with the seal of a practical mind.

It lays down one condition: keep inner silence at all times. There are ways of attaining this, at work or when alone: frequently invoking the name of Jesus, saying or singing a Psalm you know by heart, or making the simple gesture of the sign of the cross.

It is also a certain way of looking at one's neighbor, a vision transfigured by reconciliation. Anyone who is continually faced with a variety of different individuals find refreshment in these children of God; fatigue itself is swept away when they are accepted with an attentiveness constantly renewed at the wellsprings of contemplation.

Contemplative waiting upon God leads us to the acceptances necessary each day: acceptance of our state of life, our growing older, acceptance of opportunities lost. Regret itself is transformed into a dynamic act, repentance, which stimulates our advance.

In *Thomas Gordeyev*, Gorki tells how on the Volga ice destroyed Ignatius's boat. A miser who watched every rouble, he accepted the loss instantly. He knew regret would be useless, and already he felt reassured and encouraged by the thought of the new boat he was going to build.

In regret the inner self disintegrates. Far from being stimulated, a man's spirit becomes sterile when it keeps on reconstructing a situation that is past and gone, giving itself over to fruitless brooding.

Some people have had a childhood that encourages unconscious remorse. We would all like to begin over again and do better. But is there anything we do really well? We live and work in the realm of the approximate. Regret sterilizes the impulse to create. Regret debilitates.

If we are granted a time of certainty, security, and sure ground, it is when we are gathered together in contemplative waiting on God. Then, everything is possible once more. Even the salt recovers its savor; what was insipid has value again.

In contemplative waiting all our innate pessimism dissolves, even if this pessimism is rooted in what we actually see in society or in ourselves.

There are so many reasons for pessimism in the world today. There are the masses of people, increasing day by day, without any sense of God, and the Christian societies that are turned in upon themselves. There is the prospect of seeing, twenty years from now, four thousand million human beings living in deprivation, while one thousand million live in plenty. There is the huge wave slowly breaking over us: a technological civilization encapsulating man and submerging him in its totality.

There are also inner grounds for discouragement: the combat we live day after day, and the old self that refuses to submit—the pride of life, the stubborn will that persists in taking no account of its neighbor, the weight of fatigue. So many reasons in life for pessimism.

In contemplative waiting upon God everything becomes desirable again. Pessimism is watered down and yields to the optimism of faith. Then and only then is it possible to consider what is coming toward us and to welcome the events of the present time, to run toward our neighbor, to make a new start, to go forward. It is only in contemplative waiting upon God that we can find new momentum.

Wait!

Wait for the dawning of a life, when God will gather us into his arms forever.

Wait for God to act, in ourselves and in others.

Wait for a communion within the People of God, which will spark a communion among all people.

Wait for the springtime of the Church.

Wait, in spite of everything, for the spirit of mercy, for love that is not a consuming fire is not charity, and without charity we would be professing ecumenism without hope.

God is preparing for us a new Pentecost, which will set every one of us ablaze with the fire of his love. Our part is to run and meet the event that will upset all our human calculations and bring life to our dry bones.

Run toward, not away!

Run to meet mankind's tomorrow, a technological civilization fully charged with potential for human development.

Run to meet all who cannot believe, and to struggle alongside the most exploited.

Run to support a rebirth of the People of God, asking and imploring them, in season and out of season, to come together, and so to raise up in the world of men an unmistakable sign of our brotherly love.

Run toward a Christian community wearied by its long journeyings, and do everything possible to keep the ecumenical wave from falling back.

Part Two

VIOLENT
FOR
PEACE

Every one of us, Christian or not, has violence in his makeup. The only difference is in the way we use it.

Among Christians, two contradictory attitudes! For some, violence is repressed and leads to a flight from reality. The result is pietistic passivity, a lack of any involvement on behalf of the victims of injustice. Prayer is enough. Anything else might mean dirty hands.

Christians at the other extreme want destructive violence or even, if it is effective, armed force. They see no other way of registering their protest against the oppression of the poor by the powerful, especially when the oppressors employ a disguised violence.

Could there by a third way, between passivity and destructive violence? Did not Christ say that only the violent take possession of the Kingdom?[1] The Gospel spews out the lukewarm,[2] only those on fire can enter!

Everyone has to discover this third way for himself. Violence for Christ adapts itself to the age and context of each life. The road cannot be laid down in advance.

This page is taken from Brother Roger's journal. This book is interspersed with extracts from the journal. Usually they are not dated. They are not in chronological order; they were chosen to correspond to the various topics under discussion.

Why am I called to listen to so many young people violently criticizing Church institutions? Without some of these institutions there can be no continuity of Christ in our world.

Rejoice. Many young people love Christ perhaps more than in any previous age. Prophecy is not dead. Between top-heavy structures and nothing at all, another way will open up.

"That's Out of Date"

Growing Pains

In these days when the faith is being shaken to its foundations, you can find people who say about everything in the Church: "That's out of date!" They are sure that, in spite of all their reforms, the Churches still remain static.

Even for the Christian whose innermost being is unaffected, the fact that so many women and men are troubled raises a question.

To retreat into oneself and just wait would be cowardly.

To fulminate against those who reject the pillars of the faith, often for opposite reasons, would only add to the present contradictions.

We can often find no other way to express our friendship than by listening.

Listen, and keep on listening, with a heart of flesh, in order to understand. Keep your emotions in check, not out of insensitivity, but in order to leave the other free.

(JOURNAL)

It is late at night, and I am thinking over what some young people said to me today. I can still see some of their faces, the open look stamped with anxiety of one very young girl. I can still hear the harsh, serious tones of a boy speaking against the Church.

I do not doubt that they have a legitimate grievance in view of the inconsistencies of this or that Church institution. But I can sense with my whole being the turmoil this violence will arouse.

It is true that, in the past two thousand years, people have often spoken of the end of Christianity. On the eve of the year 1000, at the Renaissance, during the Enlightenment, many were convinced of it.

The number of "ex-Christians" is increasing more and more rapidly; so many, especially among the young, have left the Church in recent years. The isolation of Christians from secular man is becoming a reality.

On our hill of Taizé, I am able to talk with some of these young people. I try to discern, for myself and my contemporaries, the significance of the questions they are asking.

And the young Christians? On them, as on the others, it is impossible to pass judgment and thus discredit initiatives which may disconcert us.

It is for us, mature men and women, perhaps rich in experience, to ask ourselves where our exclusive rights come from. Even if they express themselves with violence, even if we do not always recognize ourselves in them, do we really believe that these young people are devoid of all life in Christ? The severity of older people becomes intolerable when we remember that the future of the People of God is at stake.

Intent as they are on developing new forms of Christian commitment in rapidly changing societies, it is the most normal thing in the world for young people who are searching to experience crisis situations, their "growing pains." But are there not illnesses of maturity too, maladies of those who have "made it?"

* * *

As we try to keep our ears open we sense, in the thousands of young people who pass through Taizé, contradictory aspirations. It is impossible to find any one predominant aspiration shared by them all. The chief characteristic of these young people is precisely their great diversity. Youth is multifarious. At most we might be able to distinguish two main tendencies: apathy and violence.

The apathetic. They are captivated by a few immediate interests. They are not turned toward others. Building the city of man means little to them. When they leave office or factory, all that interests them is the sporting events that come pouring from the media. Others, the well-to-do, show interest only in the pastimes of the sons and daughters of the rich. The common good, the welfare of city or state, leaves them cold, unless they treat it as just another game.

The other category is the violent. Their driving force is the will to discover the meaning of life. Some search with an honesty at times exceeding that of their elders. Others, Christian or not, translate ideas into reality right away. Some go to the point of giving their lives, and turn spontaneously toward the poorest of the poor. As for the young of the Southern hemisphere, they see, close at hand or far away, the image of our affluent societies. This oppresses them and awakens a thirst for liberation, even at the cost of violence.

Violence or revolt often express a keen desire to communicate with as many people as possible. And as far as many young Christians are concerned, their undoubted aim is to find ways of communicating with secular man. They want to live Christ with and for every human being. They long to bring everyone into the orbit of God's friendship.

Are not we, the older generation, fully in agreement with their basic aims? Why then should we cause one more break by arguing? When we pass judgment on young Christians resolutely searching, we violate their religious liberty. Forms of intransigence and narrow-mindedness bordering on intolerance are ceaselessly being reborn right at the heart of the Christian community.

(JOURNAL)

In a corner of our church, where before prayer begins I frequently talk for a moment with those who come, I listened tonight to young people outspokenly violent against Church institutions. They want to see results; they are hard on the Church, where they can see nothing but death and ruin. If they cannot see God in Christians, they cannot believe in the Church any longer.

Some of them have watered down the principles of the faith in order to facilitate encounter. For others, communion with God is an abstraction.

Confronted by such devastation, all through the liturgy, in the peace of the common prayer, tears flowed inwardly. And, in a dream, I was surprised to find myself looking forward to death, when from morning till night I marvel at the gift of life.

There is one conviction that can bring calm to troubled minds. The shaking of the faith has meant that what till then was only conformity to inherited Christianity has ripened into maturity in many young Christians. It has not meant death for all of them, but in some cases the beginning of a new life. Their violence is directed in the first place against any fossilized institutional form and against all that is not put into practice. If their intransigence sometimes turns into fanaticism, we must remember that we are living in a period of gestation.

Do we realize it? Far from being called into question, friendship with Christ makes sense to the younger generations. Not so long ago they were open to the arguments of free thought which tried to exclude Christ from the realm of reflection.

So many young Christians can no longer tolerate the wearing of masks. They would like to avoid forcing themselves into a pose where positions are exaggerated to provoke a reaction. They want to banish all artificiality, everything that inhibits the transmission of life and hinders communication.

A pessimistic reading of the events of contemporary history will always be partial. The analytic spirit lends authority. When used to pass final judgments on the young, it leads to a hopeless position.

(JOURNAL)

(June 1968) The students are demonstrating in Paris. I receive a message from which I quote these lines:

"Can you pray for us? We feel terribly alone and uncertain. We all joined together for the sake of solidarity and now we are waking up to the fact that we have been tricked on all sides, by ourselves as much as by others. No way of comprehending anything at all. We are still too brutalized by what has happened to be able to make any real sense of things.

"Talking seems useless to me. Prayer? There are times when it can't be done."

During the university demonstrations students have come to Taizé to share their experiences. Different tendencies are apparent. The great majority think things over with the earnestness typical of the new generations. Several have lost weight. They are being consumed by inner fire.

Met on three different occasions a student from the Sorbonne who took part in all the happenings in Paris in May. At first he had simply gone to have a look, nothing more.

I have known him since he was a boy. In a month he has developed unsuspected maturity.

He has rare intellectual honesty. One of the first things he said on arrival was: "In the course of the past month I could not tell when I was being artificial and when real. I was searching. After I had been beaten up, especially when I saw others being maltreated, girls included, our solidarity was automatic, it was not even conscious."

From our second conversation I have remembered these words: "What is most difficult is to understand another's motivation, to understand each other, man to man, to break out of the framework of one's own thinking."

How does he remain so serene after all he has gone through? Young people of this caliber make demands on us. Up till now they have too often been disregarded. Either we will all build a new society together or there will be two parallel societies that remain apart, and there will be nothing left for us, the older generation, but to wait for death in isolation, in the boredom and the affluence of consumer societies.

The will to repress, in a society or a group, human dignity and the rising of new life exposes that society and that group to revolt and all its consequences.

A ground swell is surging through the student world in all nations, or is about to do so. It started long ago in the universities of Latin

America. The rise in the numbers of the young gave an inkling of the growing pains we are now experiencing and which will make possible a new thrust forward.

Among students there is one constant: the rejection of a society that alienates them, the refusal to be kept during their student years in a closed human group and, as a consequence, the will to take part in decision-making. In their eyes, our society is caught up in the works of an enormous machine with names like technocracy, financial interests, the pettiness of party politics and a state of numbness brought on by overabundance.

A latent aspiration for a new society to replace a consumer economy is surfacing.

To bring in a new era Christians have a way already laid out for them: not to be swept along by events, but to stand at the crossroads.

Standing at the Heart of Tensions

In the present crisis, one of the combats that set Christians against one another lies between the two poles of minimalism and maximalism.

Though these two attitudes, also clumsily termed progressivism and integrism, may be utterly opposed, they often proceed from one and the same source. Under the pressure of an event it can happen that a Christian who has long been secure in a conservatism reverses and takes up the opposite positions. He crosses over into the camp of those who question everything—now nothing holds good for him, and nothing holds him back. How many people compensate in this way for ossified mental structures by well-constructed logical reasoning, and hide from themselves and from others a reality deep within!

Between these two extremes can be found the many who, in the spirit of poverty, are seeking a conversion of outlook. In broadening their minds, they have no other aim than to be able to communicate with as many people as possible.

They are opening a way forward. They consider that in the years to come, the further Christians advance, the more they will have to clear the ground, clinging to first principles and letting go of what is secondary.

Trying to reconcile the present with the future, they are hemmed in on all sides. This means that they must be attentive to all schools of thought, without being carried away by any one of them.

Doesn't a conversion of outlook begin as a spirit of mercy towards those whose principles differ radically from our own? Recognizing that everyone is conditioned by their upbringing. Accepting human limitations.

(JOURNAL)

A young brother pointed out to me how much our life in Taizé requires us to be attentive to a host of different factors. How right he is!

Our position constantly sets us at the heart of serious tensions. To stimulate communion in the Body of Christ, we have to listen to the aspirations of people with very different national and educational backgrounds. This necessity preserves us, I hope, from partisan choices.

Our boldness bears fruit when we use it without attacking anyone. If Pascal had left us only his Provincial Letters, he would be considered superficial and soon forgotten. That is a comforting thought in the face of all the pamphlets still to be written.

If, in order to convey clearly the great themes of the faith in the language of today, we engaged in polemics, our humanity would give place to a cold orthodoxy, entirely cerebral. It would scare people away.

(JOURNAL)

At our little council meeting this evening I was commenting on the text: "Go so far as to lay down your life for Christ's sake." And I said to my brothers: at the daily councils I never speak about our trials, the unfounded statements made about us, which we never refute in order to avoid contention. I say nothing about what causes us suffering. Why this silence? Why, on the other hand, do I mention only what is encouraging? For fear of placing a stumbling-block in someone's path. And yet, this very morning how often did I say to myself: unless the grain of wheat dies. . . .

* * *

When faced with the tensions that characterize the lives of Christians, some shut themselves up in conservatism to preserve their privileges and securities. Others believe that the novelty of certain expressions has a liberating value in itself. But are not these expressions also part of a system? Isn't a new conformity of language arising, which in its turn already needs to be demythologized?

Is there anything more dangerous than doctrinairism? How easy it is to take refuge in a system! Anyone who has imprisoned himself in that way can be recognized at once: he wants to shut others in with him. He thinks he is being carried along by a living stream, when all the time everything is gradually becoming petrified.

Anyone who is always asserting "that's out of date now!" risks being caught in his own trap. Seemingly hoping to bring about changes, he is in fact only seeking to upset things. With every advance something is automatically left behind, of course. But this expression can take on the power of a conviction strong enough to stop all life.

"That's out of date!" Perhaps this is a new cliché and, who knows, a formula which has already become a stereotype. In every age conventions have always abounded in language. It is up to us not to allow them to imprison us in new routines.

If, as some advocate, Christians were to spend their time incessantly questioning everything, what a waste of energy! Going forward does not mean for ever starting from scratch, a procedure that in any case is impossible in practice.

Our minds and bodies contain an inheritance from the recent and distant past, the mark of that early training that determines our attitudes. No one sets out in life empty-handed; we bring both assets and liabilities along with us, including the inexhaustible treasure of the perseverance of twenty centuries of faith. That counts, and we are always drawing on it to modernize our language and communication.

(JOURNAL)

Heard the details of Pope Paul VI's reception at the Chapter General of the Franciscans.

After reading a prepared message, the Pope addressed the assembly extempore: "Your way, which the younger generation with their unconventional tastes is by no means unaware of, is the way of nonconformity." To hear a Pope calling on Catholics to be nonconformists ought to fill many Protestant families with joy: they fought to hold on to that attitude.

But once nonconformity has been turned into a system, it can give rise to mistakes of the worst kind.

A nonconformist attitude demands constant revision. We soon become content to pay lip-service to a point of view, and this dispenses us from having to put it into practice.

* * *

How often does one cliché simply replace another. One wave follows another in every quickening tempo, in obedience to a contemporary trend. In our time one wave rapidly submerges the previous one. What explanation will they have for man in the year 2000?

The notion "secular man" is already being called into question. Didn't an atomic physicist tell me that among his colleagues, he had discovered only two who could truly be called atheists? A small number consider themselves Christians, but all are searching.

It is so true that there is no conflict between secular life and prayer. On the contrary, they are related.

Secularization helps people to rediscover the meaning of the provisional. It can become a positive value and set free forces that have been held back: there are forms of peity, expressions of prayer, a style of Church institutions that alienate, keeping us from communion with God and man.

Between that and unreserved infatuation with the march toward secularization, there is a world of difference. It would be naive optimism. . . .

In the first place it has become clear that all radical desacralization leads to a resacralization in nonreligious terms. Human beings cannot bear a vacuum. They fill it up with a resurgence of the sacred that has been abolished. They create ceremonies, solemn inaugurations, medals, banners. . . .

In the second place, it is easy to end up in secularism. Secularism is another system. It aims at exorcising idols but, far from succeeding, it leaves a person empty, alienates his freedom, takes away his thirst for communion. And then some call for a "religionless" Christianity. For them, prayer is just monologue. Countering a traditional formulation that says that God is to be found only in a vertical relationship, they claim to find him only in other human beings, in the horizontal dimension. They locate God in the depths of the soul, in communication with others, and nowhere else. We need only go down deep enough into ourselves to find him.

But have we not brilliantly succeeded, once again, in imprisoning God in a particular terminology? What do these new expressions accomplish besides shifting around the terms? At one time God was perceived only in the heights, and today he is supposed to be only in the depths of the personality.

Fortunately God exceeds our categories. Christ descended into the depths of the earth[3] to give to all who came before him the possibility of knowing him.[4] At the same time he descended into every single human being. But he ascended, too. He is located in all dimensions—height, depth, and breadth.[5] If we are attentive, we shall discover him at all the crossroads of our lives.

(JOURNAL)

For our part we have been discovering in recently years that, with young people, systematic desacralization dissolves of its own accord as they participate in the common prayer.

*Why do they come and pray with us? The fact that many of my
brothers are called to live for a time amongst the poorest of the
poor awakens a positive reaction in many of them. It is in an equal-
ly impossible situation, amidst the apathy of so many, that these
young people in their turn will have to persevere.*

What's the Use of Praying?

Affluent societies impose a life of boredom. There is no longer the
same need to fight for existence; a certain lassitude takes hold of
people. Everything is guaranteed from the start, which means a life
of mediocrity.

So the same questioning arises everywhere, and it is heard on the
lips of many Christians: "What's the use?"

Often the question is put to me: "What's the use of praying
when we know about the terrible suffering, disease, war, and, still
present in our memories, the terror in the eyes of millions of children, women and men, pushed into the gas ovens?"

(JOURNAL)

*A young brother wrote me these lines just after plunging into the
life of a shanty-town of Recife, in the northeast of Brazil, where no
one ever knows what tomorrow will bring: "In the face of all that
can be seen, we must constantly work to keep a balance in order to
temper the reactions aroused by injustice. There are questions you
cannot help but ask: if God exists, why evil? If God is good, why
suffering? If God is good and omnipotent, why humiliation and
hatred? There is no definitive explanation. We must look for an
answer in the life we are living."*

*Another young brother, on his return from one of our frater-
nities, spoke to me of the apparent uselessness of their life sub-
merged in the midst of Chicago's black ghetto. What can a few
Christians with scanty resources accomplish in such enormous,
highly organized modern societies, feverishly in search of profit?
And now brothers are back from Africa talking in similar terms.*

The uselessness of my life: that is the cry welling from the depths of
the great majority.

They wonder about the meaning of their life. What has it contributed to mankind? Failure takes some parents by surprise in their declining years. They loved their children to the extent of founding a family cell living in a private happiness all its own. Then an incident occurred, perhaps the revolt of an idolized offspring, and the result is devastating catastrophe.

Anyone who has devoted himself blindly to another person can be overtaken by the impression of never having done enough. The need to sacrifice, which has become intense, predominates.

Does anyone really believe that their life has been of some use? And who could claim to be fully useful? At the heart of the fullest possible life, we remain poor servants[6] but, at the same time, co-workers with God.[7] There is no contradiction in the dialectic of the Gospel. Those who sow in tears of uselessness harvest in song. One day blossoms appear and inward joy. Then the blossom falls and, after a time of waiting, the fruit. A whole lifetime is barely enough.

The extreme of perseverance consists in gratuitous giving, even if this has little meaning for members of an affluent society: they want successes, but no sooner are they achieved than satsifaction disappears, to be replaced by the hunt for new triumphs.

(JOURNAL)
The impression of being useless can be very real for everybody. I have just met a man who asserted that he had never in his life experienced a single victory. I read in him an expression of self-effacement, full of sorrow. No sooner had he closed the door than I hastened to write to him words that I had been unable to say: "Can honest men ever succeed in the battle of the business world? You are a man of infinite honesty. Your victory lies in the unlimited confidence people who really know you have in you. I remain close to you, praying a poor prayer."

* * *

As far as we are concerned there are days when, to prevent us from falling into routine, I would like to see a notice nailed to the door of the church: "The form of our common prayer is continually evolving."

But if I went as far as to say of prayer itself "that's out of date," it would be better to have closed up shop altogether. Prayer will never be outdated. It pertains to a realm of communication beyond our control.

Young people pray, today more than ever. And at times this can even upset those mature men who project upon the young their own impossibilities.

(JOURNAL)

A monk asked me why, in Taizé, so many young people enter so deeply into the prayer. I told him that just recently, an experience that astonished us happened on two separate occasions. A group of young people was present at the prayer for the first time and then went away. The next day, they retraced their steps and came back here to spend the few days they had reserved for going to the seaside.

The same experience occurred with another group, a week later, although the two groups had not been in contact with each other. A few hours after leaving, back they came for several more days.

I asked them why. Their response: they were searching for God. For them, what was essential here was the common prayer. Why? Because it is continued day after day by men in whom they sense a real commitment.

But in addition to this, is not common prayer an event in which time has a different quality, in which it becomes charged with the weight of eternity? In prayer, all of us together are momentarily lifted out of time. And that is what matters for modern man, caught up in the demands of a society based on productivity and technology.

Could praying with so many young people ever make us forget adults? Nothing could be further from the truth. Anyone who has known how to listen to the old has often received a treasure.

And, at certain times of the year, when children join us for prayer, that is another complementary sign. All the generations together, bearing a living word.

There as elsewhere, reciprocities play their part. If a community like ours can persevere day after day, it is because of the faithfulness of so many women, men, and children. They are there, present with us, and they support us.

Whatever our situation, none of us are privileged. Every day we have to take up afresh the dialogue with God and learn how to pray all over again.

Some days, everything is said in few words. At other times everything is long drawn out, and we are in danger of reeling off meaningless clichés. Accept the fact that, our whole life long, we will be constantly having to learn to pray all over again. How many discoveries lie before us, and what a freshness in having to keep on searching!

As he grows older, man acquires certainty. It is anchored within him, even if it does not cover the whole of his personality. With the passage of years, this certainty takes on increasing importance. The "I believe" is what counts. But never do we acquire the privilege of not having to add in the same breath "help my unbelief."[8]

(JOURNAL)

Conversation with some monks. I attempt to explain our solidarity with them. Perhaps they do not feel at home in our common prayer? And yet we have invented nothing; we have simply adapted the prayer of the ages.

Besides, everyone gets out of it what they can. Our common prayer is like a mosaic—beautiful for some, shapeless for others. What has no meaning for one speaks to another. One appreciates the Psalms, or the long silences after the Scripture readings, or the litanies. There are some who look forward especially to the music or the singing at the end of the common prayer.

Each has their piece of cake. To imagine that everything could be understood with equal intensity, even if only by one individual, is wishful thinking.

* * *

How could anyone say "what's the use?" regarding the simple presence of Christians all over the world? People are always free to choose God or to decide to despise their neighbor. But the presence of Christians can overturn determinisms of brutality and hatred. They reestablish relationship with God. They have the audacity, in the continuity of their prayer, to be ever turning to a source of refreshment.

(JOURNAL)

Reflecting on meeting Christ on the last day, a meeting I do not dread, I found myself writing: What will I be asked in that first face-to-face encounter about which I know nothing much, except that it will be the first of many, for an unlimited length of time?

Some are perhaps right to say that every representation of ultimate realities is premature. Nevertheless, I have tried to answer my own question and I have imagined the dialogue. Won't I hear myself saying:

". . . as for the community, I loved something about it that not many people would guess. They appreciated Taizé for its openness, for its dialogue with so many different people. More than this sharing, the waiting in contemplation was what I considered most valuable.

"You suffered. You also desired to live the Gospel's call to chastity. You tried to be signs of the timeless among men and for them, signs to be reinvented and renewed each day.

"This waiting took place independently of any intellectual gifts. It was possible for each one, even for those who considered themselves quite untalented. Waiting in contemplation was more valuable than anything else.

"Yes, the essential was the inner combat, lived out each day in a new beginning."

Life Commitment Called Into Question

Many are afraid of making a commitment for life. They want to live events without the faithfulness of an entire lifetime, a today with no continuity, the provisional and nothing else.

This is particularly true of the Gospel call to celibacy.

(JOURNAL)

A pastor inquired what had caused us the most suffering. The hardest thing to bear was the intolerance, particularly from our own Churches.

Why, from the very beginning, the refusal to consider as a vocation the yes pronounced for life in response to a call? After a lapse of over four centuries since the Reformation, we wanted to live in celibacy. But how many times have we had to listen to the argument: you cannot imprison the freedom of the Holy Spirit in a commitment for life.

At the beginning, we renewed our commitment to celibacy once a year. Then we realized that the Holy Spirit was strong enough to bind for life men who, for Christ's sake, desired to live permanently in the state in which the call came to them.[9]

At first we were far from realizing the full significance of this gift. Long afterwards we made the discovery that it leaves us free and open for everyone.

I ought to mention here a fact that was significant for me personally. Shortly before my first communion, I had made an attempt to persuade my father, a pastor, to postpone the date. But he could not face the reproach of having a son who refused an obligation everyone else accepted. At Easter all boys and girls of sixteen, without exception, made their first communion.

In the end I had to bow to his wishes. I felt he was doing his duty, and I preferred to ignore the cost to myself.

On the day I made my first communion, my father chose for me this text from the Gospel: "Be faithful unto death and I will give you the crown of life."[10]

It was only much later that I paid any attention to it. Perhaps that living word has not returned to God void.[11]

Can someone who has become a sign of contradiction by his commitment to celibacy decide to stop being a living word? Is he not called instead to keep alive within himself an attitude of waiting upon God, and a relationship with him?

He can only achieve this by living Christ for others. Otherwise chastity becomes a burden, the burden of someone who is merely filling a sociological role.

If the values of contemplation have gradually dried up, chastity crumbles, and every final, once-and-for-all privation leads inevitably either to passivity or to revolt.

(JOURNAL)
At my table, a friend of long standing, a Protestant layman of exceptional open-mindedness. He informed me that one of his pupils was about to marry a priest who was leaving his order after twelve years of life in community.

Then the subject changed and the conversation continued. But I was numb with dismay. Our sensibilities could not be in harmony—he, with his teaching responsibilities, and I, the brother of my brothers.

What would I not give up to help people reflect on their first decision and rediscover a way of being faithful until death to the commitment they have made?

During the Second Vatican Council, I was sharply made aware that the unity of the Catholic Church would endure in spite of all possible reforms, except one. She would break in two if priests already committed to celibacy were authorized to marry. After a thousand years in which the priesthood and celibacy were closely bound up with one another, susceptibilities would be wounded to the quick. Catholics on the whole are not prepared for a change of this kind.

And yet, no one is blind to the fact that, in some places, chastity is at times impossible for priests living in isolation, even if they are afire with their pastoral vocation. How often do I find myself thinking of those men!

* * *

For many young people sexuality is no longer taboo. When they use it indiscriminately, with no restraints, they devalue it.

In compensation, other impulses are set free, forces of aggression.

Being fully human means recognizing all these components of our being. Knowledge of one's make-up is of prime importance for anyone who wants to offer himself every day anew.

How can we tap all the forces within us, the emotions, the unfathomable depths seething with manifold and unsuspected energies? How can we put all this at the disposal of Christ, in full awareness of what we are offering? In this regard, a man who chooses celibacy allows himself to be affected in the very depths of his being when he makes such an intensely personal offering. He is seeking to encounter the Risen Christ, in order to go out and encounter every human being.

Once this vocation has taken hold of him, he lives it out his whole life long, by day and in the watches of the night, in solitude and through days of greyness. He is well aware of the absolute this encounter implies.

Never since the Reformation has the Catholic priesthood been shaken to such an extent. Some feel that celibacy is the reason. There are psychiatrists who assert that this is not the only cause. "It is no secret that the celibate's situation brings with it tensions, frustrations, and problems. We must not forget that the marital situation brings with it no fewer problems, although they are of a radically different order. To put it simply, it would be naive to suppose that a human being can only be happy in marriage and that an unmarried person is inevitably unhappy and unbalanced. This somewhat juvenile generalization is sharply contradicted by experience."[12]

The present crisis concerns, above all, the ministry. In Protestantism, where the clergy are nearly all married, the upheaval is just as great. It is expressed in violent reaction against any attempt to identify the ministry with an ecclesiastical status. In the course of centuries a clerical system has grown up, in Protestantism as elsewhere. Today, pastors and priests are trying to determine what is specific to this ministry. They refuse to be mere functionaries.

(JOURNAL)

I remember along with so many other pastors' sons, what it means to have experienced as a child a situation of being different, to have been branded as a member of a "caste." Recently I have been putting the question of a married diaconate to couples actively involved in the Church. In general their reply can be summed up as follows: how can we avoid creating a new clerical system that will imprison the children in an ecclesiastical environment?

Entertained some pastors from Geneva at my table. Among them some young men who did not disguise their anxiety. They said: "There is nothing more debilitating than to be looked upon as religious functionaries. The pastoral duties that have to be done, baptisms, marriages, funerals, become an intolerable burden in the end. Why are we prohibited from earning our living like everyone else? The time devoted to the ministry would then become more intense."

* * *

I have never prepared myself so much for a 29th of June. On that day many priests are ordained. Among them, friends of mine.

They are entering a minstry at a very young age. They will have to face a society which has no interest in their commitment. They will no longer find in the Church the protection of belonging to a people, a firm support in bygone days.

They will know the ebb and flow of the years, discouragement, weariness, and the renunciation of sparkling hopes.

Only holiness will be able to open a way for them during an entire lifetime. Without it, they will withdraw into themselves or seek all kinds of compensations. Holiness alone will link them directly to Christ and to all the witnesses of the faith.

The provincial of an order has just spent two days here. He was on his way home from Niger where he lived near a Taizé fraternity. He said to one of my brothers, who had graduated from engineering college and was working as a mason on a building site, "By your work you are contributing to human development."

The brother's answer struck him: "The people here do not know what a Christian is. Our first aim is to live the holiness of Christ. All the rest, sharing in human development, is a necessary consequence."

Community Life Under Trial by Fire

As regards the monastic vocation, some say that it too is out of date. They ask searching questions:

Why do members of religious communities often postpone necessary changes?

Why do they bring suffering on themselves by separating old and young? They are no longer a sign of brotherhood and community, and can only bemoan the indifference shown to them.

What has become of the men who began by consecrating themselves in commitment for life, with a view to being available for all?

(JOURNAL)

A few days ago, a priest assured me that the monastery where he had spent some time had no future. And yet, when institutions are worn out, it is still possible to count on the men and women who animate them. In the event, I am convinced, because I know him, that the man in charge of this monastery is capable of reviving his whole community.

Every change in human nature works from within. It is from within that our mental structures are modified. It is in the secret places of the heart that continuous conversion to Christ takes place —the Christ we are continually forgetting, and continually denying.

Of course we must do all in our power to reform antiquated structures. If such structures are not animated by men of generous heart, however, reforms may make them look better, they will have the merit of logical consistency, but they will shed no light.

To another friend I was explaining the drama of the Reformation. At a given moment, despair at not seeing reforms coming within Catholicism gained the upper hand. Some wanted to move ahead without their brothers. God allowed his Spirit to breathe upon this new creation: he loves his own too much to abandon them. But the image of the unity of the Body of Christ faded away.

These days, life in community is undergoing trial by fire, but its rebirth through solidarity with the laity can already be foreseen. They are channels of exceptional vitality.

A part of the laity is unshaken by the present crisis. Among other things, these lay people believe in a vocation to contemplation. Their high standards and courageous commitments enable many priests and pastors to hold fast in the midst of the turmoil. Their healthy reaction will often sustain vocations which, without this support, would have foundered in revolt or defeatism.

Without reciprocity between committed lay people and those characterized by a vocation to contemplation, no fullness is possible for either group. If solidarity were maintained only among the laity, or only among "religious," an irreplaceable ecumenical dimension would disappear.

For the laity, fascinated by technology, formed by the world of the image, religious communities can be as never before a sign of eternity.

But on their side, there are some members of communities who go to live, a few at a time, at the heart of the masses, to enrich their vocation to community life. For them, the alternation between life in a small fraternity in the inner city, and regular returns to the roots of their family life, to the site of their community, is a source of equilibrium.

(JOURNAL)
Recently, the presence among us of the "spiritual families" of Charles de Foucauld gave us the opportunity to review the friendship that has always existed between us.

Had the unity of the Church been a reality when Taizé first began, we would not have hesitated: the Little Brothers and Little Sisters of Father de Foucauld were closest to our own aspirations at that time. But because of our ecumenical vocation, we took different paths.

The time came when we had to emerge from silence to welcome others, in particular, young people.

And in another connection, at the time when we were starting, a woman expressed her firm conviction, just before she died, that dispersal of all the brothers in fraternities would work against that visible sign of community to which Christians could refer. In a world where everything invites us to scatter, this sign remains essential. Perhaps that woman had a presentiment of the conditions of life today that are dislocating people and societies, and impel them to come to a community for times of re-creation.

* * *

Some suppose that we at Taizé are in a privileged position with respect to Church institutions, as if the margin of freedom were greater here than elsewhere.

It is correct that we have refused to create movements and institutions dependent upon us. There are, however, relationships that endure. They limit our freedom. They oblige us not to build without others.

At some periods of our life, the range of freedom shrinks, only to widen again later. We have to accept that we build within limits which are more or less defined.

When the limits come closer and the scope for building together becomes narrower, we could fall prey to disappointment. Day by day we take heart again as we make use of an area that is limited, but still offers room for creativity.

Within the People of God, nothing can be built apart from the limitations implied in our solidarity with the whole body. This is a part of our vocation to live out the catholicity of the Church.

(JOURNAL)

Spent an evening which will perhaps have been the most memorable of the entire year. I entertained friends from Poland. The con-

*versation flowed along peacefully until the moment I heard them
say that in the great difficulties of their life, in the balance they
seek to maintain between Marxists and the Church, they constantly refer to a small contemporary community that sustains their
hope.*

*To hear such a strong assertion about oneself arouses astonish-
ment and embarrassment. And I am not even reporting all they
said.*

It led me to summon all my brothers together and say:

*Who are we? A gathering of men who did not choose one
another and who are trying to relive something of the first Christian community.*

*Who are we? A small, fragile community, kept going by an irra-
tional hope: the reconciliation of all Christians and of all humanity; a community of Christians called upon to accomplish tasks far
beyond their powers but who, in spite of their limited numbers, try
to respond to the appeals that come to them from all sides.*

*Nothing at all would happen if we were not, first and foremost,
a community of men who persevere, each within himself, in a combat that can be very trying, for Christ and for him alone.*

*One day, the pride of life could seep into us, and what was pure-
ly response to a call would dissolve. Something would inevitably
fill the vacuum: a need for power, a kind of triumphant assertion
of the self, aggression toward everything that in any way stands for
the original call.*

*Persevere! That is one of the themes that daily strikes an an-
swering chord within us, in a period of history when more and
more is being called into question. We could not keep going in an
atmosphere of continuous fireworks. They would blind us and
keep us from living in reality. If it is good that from to time one of
these fireworks should come and brighten our lives, that is because
it helps us to return, untiringly, to perseverance.*

*So who are we? A small community, sometimes shaken to its
foundations. But always rising again, because borne by a Presence
greater than itself, which links it to the eternal.*

*Who are we? If our present situation had to be summed up in a
few words: we are an accumulation of personal weaknesses, but a
community visited by One other than ourselves.*

A Way Out

New Rifts

This century, called the "century of ecumenism," is it really the century of a communion?

In recent years splits, oppositions, and new divisions have been appearing everywhere. The rift between a Northern hemisphere, oversaturated with ideas, with its affluent societies, and a Southern hemisphere becoming poorer and poorer, with vast explosive regions which refuse to be a by-product of the West. A rift in theology. A rift between the generations.

Why this absence of peace in the People of God?

Peace is lost when, in the old and new divisions between Christians, we instinctively focus on the errors of the other. This makes us incapable of approaching our counterpart to say:

I wanted to make the People of God purer, more uncompromising, freer of the burden of the years and the weight of the centuries. But I could not do so, for I was acting without you. What I thought had been purified in my community had in fact lost out in impact in the community of mankind.

How can we become aware that in every rift, as in every divorce, both sides always share responsibility?

Since the first centuries, Christians have been exhorting one another to peace in this way: "Begin the work of peace within yourself so that with peace in your own heart, you are able to bring peace to others."[13]

Without this principle, anchored at the heart of the Christian vocation, everything is in turmoil. Everything, even ecumenism, can become a ferment of opposition, among those who are holding back reforms as well as among those who wish for change. Some

of them have suffered in the People of God. They were unable, in
burning patience, to cope with their trials.

How is it that this "century of ecumenism" is not by now the
century of a communion?

Could it be that in the West, the habit formed over more than
four centuries of wielding anathemas at one another has halted the
dynamism of openness, good will, and the spirit of forgiveness?

The conviction that we are in the right leads us to pass judgments on Christians who are not like ourselves. Could this be hin-
dering us from allowing prayer for all, even for those who discredit
us, to enter into our hearts?

When we judge others we are obeying, in spite of ourselves, a
law written into our very nature and not only valid for Christians,
a law of guilt: an agnostic writer asserted that it had taken him a
year of depression to purge twenty-five years of latent guilt.

Communion between Christians, like that of the conjugal cell or
of any other community, is not obtained by forcing others to fulfill
certain demands. There is nothing more destructive of the personality than paying attention to our neighbor for the sole purpose of
reforming him.

(JOURNAL)
*A friend questions me: "You believe in facts. But why then does
no negative evaluation come from your pen, no criticism of the
facts, whether with regard to Protestantism or to Catholicism?"*

I replied:

*Never forget that we are emerging from an ancient history made
up of centuries of misunderstanding. A particular sensibility has
been created, mental processes formed. So many mutual judgments have been passed between Christians of various confessions.
They do not lead to a change of attitude in the other, nor do they
bring about the desired modifications.*

*In the situation in which we find ourselves, to protest in order to
set the other on the road that seems best to us can only close his
mind instead of opening it.*

For my part, my burning desire is never to cast anathemas on anyone at all. This does not mean condoning error, but finding the right time to speak.

There is a pedagogy of discretion, which brings into play the vital forces of the personality. Man only really becomes himself when he is trusted. It is only when there is trust that everything can be said.

Welcoming others in an atmosphere of boundless good will allows dialogue, one day, to turn into sharing. Once begun with Christians, it widens to include agnostics or nonbelievers.

*　*　*

It is easy to find an explanation for the intolerance of some majority Churches. But where does the intolerance of certain Christian minorities come from? Where does this lack of respect for the individual come from, at the first sign of any thinking outside the expected conformity?

A sociological law is at work here. A minority is afraid of being absorbed, and so it rejects all pressure toward unity.

Whether the minorities are Catholic or Protestant, the process is identical. They can only partially appreciate the vocations of others. They analyze all that comes to their attention with a view to protecting themselves against it.

They are the heirs of previous generations and, though they may sometimes be in opposition to their own fathers, the sons are infected with a virus of intolerance no less violent than that of their forebears. The motivations may be entirely different; the phenomenon remains the same.

(JOURNAL)

A French priest told me how much easier it was for him to enter into relationship with pastors and laity from a Church in another country, which has been the majority Church from its very beginning. It is much easier to go further in discussions with them. On the other hand, Protestants who feel they are placed in an inferior position by the overwhelming numbers of Catholics tend to keep their distance.

Some are astonished that, geographically situated as it is in the French confessional context, Taizé has escaped criticism. It is true that we have never had to bear attacks on our moral integrity. Nonetheless, there has been significant opposition to some of the directions we have taken.

Some Protestants have become more aloof, but at the same time some Catholics have reacted to us with apprehension because we stemmed from the Reformation.

As sons of two families, we are heirs of a four-centuries-old divorce. We want to reconcile our paternal family, that of our fathers, the Churches of the Reformation, with our mother Church, the Catholic Church. We shall never be able to pass judgments on the one to allay the fears of the other. We would never want to say anything to wound the love we bear to either.

And now that we have Catholic brothers we live more than ever this new reality, the reality of a double allegiance.

(JOURNAL)

A few days ago, after answering questions from a group representing some thirty nations, I wanted in my turn to ask for their impressions of us. They considered the matter. This is what they replied: Is it correct to see in your community on the one hand a vocation to suffering, and at the same time the freshness of the Gospel? If so, we have only one thing to say, stay as you are.

In some parts of the world, ecumenism has experienced a tremendous thrust forward. It has led to a real improvement in relations between separated Christians.

Still, that is no reason for euphoria. Young Christians feel bound to express their uneasiness and dissent. If ecumenism is just another idea, what's the good of it? If it does not lead, here and now, to concrete steps forward, it loses its importance.

Can anything that does not lead to communion in the Body of Christ and the building up of the city of man possibly continue to be of any interest to us?

Too many dialogues lead nowhere. They have their place, but there comes a time when cooperation and coming together are necessary.

The most balanced among the young people say:

When we speak or act as Christians, we do with respect to a confessional family; we take a localized history as our point of reference. Entangled as we are, then, we want an ecumenism which allows us to live with today as our starting point.

Can ecumenism possibly be anything but an institution with no future, if some assert: we have been separated for centuries, so it will take centuries for us to achieve communion?

We are looking for communion in the near future.

With Pope John XXIII, we assert that we don't want to put history on trial to determine who was wrong and who was right.[14]

We don't want to remain imprisoned in a limited vision that sees everything in function of our own local history.

We want to live Christ for others and, through a communion among Christians, to stimulate friendship among all.

We can no longer tolerate confessional segregation; it is just as hypocritical as racial segregation.

We are aware of the virus with which our Christian societies have been infected. For four hundred years now, its name has been: self-defense, self-justification, controversy. It leads ever anew to a process of withdrawal inward, which can make ecumenism just one more institution, channeled into the many and various Churches and in its turn encouraging further withdrawal inwards. This virus neutralizes and even blocks everything that impels us to move toward other people and towards catholicity.

We will not make ecumenism into one more ideology, a good topic for conferences in which everyone will go on justifying their own positions for ever and ever.

For us ecumenism is neither an idea nor a notion; it is a response of faith to an event of God in our history.

(JOURNAL)
Some theology students assure me they can no longer keep going within the present structures. They ask me: What can we create to find a way out of the impasse?

I look at them. One of them, Pierre, looks to me to be the personification of levelheadedness. In another I sense a disillusionment that has already descended to the depths of his personality.

I try to answer them. It is only possible to find a way through a crisis in the context in which it first met us.

* * *

The fragmentations currently taking place will have for Christians consequences just as formidable as the rupture in the sixteenth century, unless women and men arise who are determined to make fresh advances.

There is no hope for them to be bearers of peace if they are not, first and foremost, men and women of an encounter, that encounter which takes place, through the watches of our nights and throughout our days, with that Man among men, Jesus Christ.

Remarkable, this encounter in the heart of every human being.

But it is impossible to stop there. Soon the need for encounter with man makes itself felt, even with those who do not share our faith or who opppose it.

In the features of every person, especially when tears and suffering have made them more transparent, it becomes possible to contemplate the face of Christ himself.

The Dynamic of Catholicity

Catholic—the name itself is a challenge. Catholic, ecumenical, universal are synonyms. Anyone who bears this name has much to live up to: to be catholic, open to all that concerns humanity.

A universal solidarity, involving all human beings, is more imperative than ever. Without it, no hope for peace on earth, nor of human development for everybody.

And yet now, in the heart of the Catholic Church, new divisions are arising.

Who would deny the urgent need for a confrontation? In a dialogue that touches the depths of the personality, it becomes possible for each one to understand the other's point of view, the whys and wherefores of his choices.

Confrontation requires clear thinking and vigorous analysis. It allows us to grasp the motivations behind this or that line of thought. Some, aware of the power of secularization that influences every Christian, have been given the mission to awaken people more and more to a sense of the eternal. Others, on the contrary, participate as far as possible in the combats of contemporary man.

Tensions become creative if everyone goes beyond his own limitations to understand what the Spirit is saying to the Church through others than himself. Dialogue is enriched when each makes an effort to understand the appeals addressed to Christians involved in a different mission, but wholeheartedly committed to serving people the world over.

Diversity of viewpoints guarantees freedom and is stimulating. It makes for fruitful dialogue. But when the confrontation loses sight of its goal, when concern for mankind as a whole disappears, the temptation arises for each person to retreat to the "right" side of the fence and pour criticism upon those whose mission is different.

(JOURNAL)

We are more or less humiliated according to whether we have taken risks or not: every courageous step inevitably brings criticism.

But too much humiliation can wear us down. And then even the man most firmly rooted in Christ is tempted to look for purely psychological compensations.

When people assert that, however violent the oppositions between Catholics, this is not an age of schisms (and I am firmly convinced of that), along with many others I reply: in the light of its fundamental vocation to catholicity, is not so much hardness of heart going to lead to indifference those who are looking to the Catholic Church?

(JOURNAL)

Learn to wait until opposing points of view come together: how many times did I repeat that to myself during the Second Vatican Council!

Being plunged into an assembly like that was a real endurance test. I had prepared myself for it. And yet I prefer to live on a more human scale, here at Taizé, supported by community prayer, rather than being catapulted into an assembly of such vast proportions, even if it is the most fascinating of adventures.

An adventure! We were even more conscious of that toward the end. As the closing days drew near, tensions rose in proportion to the importance of the decisions. Weren't we all cherishing the very human desire to see our own thinking reflected in the documents?

Nothing could be less ecumenical! What has not grown out of a common endeavor cannot be imposed, otherwise we would simply be burdening others with our own singularities.

For a long time, the Catholic Church believed it was her duty to maintain her unity by means of all the firmness she could muster. Was that to the detriment of solidarity with all?

This attitude is changing rapidly. Earlier many barriers were erected. People today cannot stand barriers any longer; they do not take the time to see what is behind them. Even if the barriers set up have no other aim than to protect one of the values of the Church, they are counterproductive. Legalistic expressions are a stumbling block. We need to find a new language, relevant to contemporary man.

Not that we have to call into question the fundamentals of the faith. But when the fundamentals are expressed in a new language, our horizons open out to unimaginable dimensions: communion in the faith remains, but intransigence dominates no longer.

I rejoice in the use of modern languages in the liturgy of today, but I know that is not enough to keep it from becoming mechanical.

Sometimes I worry about the over-rapid reading of the Bible during the common prayer. As if the passages were "magic words" which have to be recited but not understood. Nowadays people are not good at remembering what is read to them. Or am I being too severe, forgetting that crumbs always fall from the table?

Surely there have always been people of the word and people of contemplation in the Church. At close quarters, a deep gulf seems to separate them. Seen in perspective, they are nourished by the same bread.

When we agree on the Church values that bring Christ to a greater number of people, our minds expand to a more universal dimension; they "become catholic."

Who is more attentive to his neighbor than a man or a woman who is truly catholic? Everything can find room in their heart of hearts: concern for every human situation, the prayer of the Church thoughout the ages and its contemporary realization, tears for someone in trouble and joy for someone thankful for today. They are capable of a passionate concern for unity, no matter what the cost: not in dreams but in existing Churches which, by a law of sociology, are always tempted to put the interests of the local situation first, and thus slow down the dynamic of catholicity.

Courageous Gestures

Though there are places where ecumenism has taken gigantic strides forward, elsewhere approaches are still timid. There are countries where, on this topic, there is total silence. While some have not yet begun the first stammerings of dialogue, others are far beyond that stage.

It is important to offer concrete possibilities to those who are advancing. How else can we emerge from a dead end that will not fail to lead the young either to violence or to apathy? When dialogue has made an encounter possible, the time comes when a new stage is imperative, that of action. To refuse this is to run the risk of limiting oneself to a sentimental ecumenism, where all that matters is for separated Christians to open their hearts to each other and love one another.

As long as dialogue is making progress, the dead end is less apparent. But what disillusionment when we are forced to admit that a relationship which has brought us closer without uniting us has wasted precious time! It is honest to say that, by itself, dialogue is not potent enough to lead to communion. How then can we find a way out?

A new step that could be taken to bring consummation nearer would be to recognize the unity that already exists in countless cells, even provisional ones, in the Church throughout the world.

Comfortably settled in our parallel histories, we have no illusion about a unity initiated as the result of negotiation or legal agreements. Unity will be recognized when it has appeared. Then the Churches with enough courage and magnanimity will modify the texts and structures that are no longer in tune with reality.

(JOURNAL)

Tedious conversation. A questioner wants to know what distinguishes Protestantism from Catholicism. I take my courage in both hands to answer him, even though a voice within me says: move on.

Nearly three hundred Protestant denominations: you would have to be an expert to find your bearings! What is distinctive in Protestantism? To simplify matters, I base my answer upon what we are living here in Taizé.

One of our brothers, from a Protestant Church in northern Europe, never saw the Eucharist celebrated facing the congregation before coming to Taizé.

Another was taught as a child to make the sign of the cross.

Another was brought up to go to confession and drew from absolution the strength needed for living.

Another, also a Protestant, saw celebrations of the Eucharist with the ancient vestments—chasuble, stole, crozier, and mitre for the bishop, candles burning before the curcifix and on the altar. In his Church, ordinary bread was never used, only hosts.

Yet another brother, less typical, was taught by his father, a minister, to venerate the Virgin Mary.

Casting an eye over the diversity of Protestantism, we can see that none of those things are characteristic, but all of them belong to it. Where then is the line of demarcation? The crucial point is certainly still the refusal to accept the ministry of the Pope and the most recent dogmas on the Virgin.

* * *

Still now, I often refer to the conversation I had with myself when, as a young man, I rediscovered the faith. I found it hard to understand some people's views on the Communion. For some it meant merely meeting together in memory of Christ. Others saw it simply as a fraternal meal.

As I had been brought up on the Scriptures since I was a child, I compared two texts. The first: "When two or three meet together in my name, I am with them."[15] The second: "This is my body; this is my blood."[16] I said to myself: if I meet with a few Christians, he is present; he promised, and I take his word for it. But if I receive the bread and wine of the Eucharist, that is a different presence, which incorporates me into the Risen Christ. If not, what is the good of this meal?

When he says, "This is my body," Christ is speaking of a presence entirely different from his spiritual presence promised to two or three who meet in his name.

When we live from the real presence of Christ in the Eucharist, we are sustained by a faith that does not belong to us. To reject it would perhaps dispose people to understand us better, but would that be the Gospel?

We will need infinite courage and realism to discern unity and adapt ourselves to it. The documents will come later. To make courageous gestures in this regard, heavy responsibilities rest on the two great ancient Churches, the Orthodox and the Catholic. They existed before the divorce. They can retard or they can promote much.

The Eastern Church is seeking her own unity, in a complicated context. But she has the possibility of showing ways to relationships between sister-Churches.

We in the West are waiting for our mother Church, the pre-Reformation Catholic Church, to be reconciled with our paternal family, which transmitted the faith to us through our fathers.

This is why, if we want to make this communion a reality, we are at the very heart of a dilemma: even with a view to a more universal communion, we simply cannot break with our own family of origin. Rejection is not part of the dynamic of modern man. For the period of transition, can we accept the possibility of a "double allegiance"? Will we have enough imagination and courage to reconstitute our unity without asking anyone for a denial of his forebears, and so become ferments of communion in the entire community of mankind throughout the inhabited world?

In this situation—many are more or less aware of it—there is one Christian who perhaps has the means of leading us out of this dead end. In the sixteenth century, one pope condemned. In his ministry of communion, could today's Bishop of Rome be audacious enough to propose a "double allegiance," without suggesting that anyone deny the faith transmitted to him in all sincerity by his ancestors? It would be unthinkable that a Church whose vocation it is to be universal and catholic should exclude anyone.

It is a courageous step of this sort that we dare to ask for, with the violence of peacemakers.

(JOURNAL)

Rome. Conversation at table with theologians considered traditional. The best qualified among them began to talk about the ways to unity:

If sometimes there is a rift between Catholic and Protestant the-ologies, rifts just as deep exist between different Catholic schools of thought. The difference between Thomist and Franciscan or Augustinian schools of thought is just as great as between the posi-tions of Luther and Saint Thomas Aquinas.

And so it is possible to hope: if they consent to be com-plementary, different tendencies can coexist in a true communion, not only between East and West, but among Western Christians themselves.

Another courageous gesture. Will it be possible much longer to seek communion among Christians without accepting the ministry of a pastor of pastors and communities, who embodies in himself the service of mercy?

It would scarcely be realistic to imagine that one day the Catholic Church will abandon this ministry that has come down through the ages, purifying itself on its way.

Who would not rejoice at the attention paid to a Christian able to forge ahead and be, in the name of the vast majority, a pro-moter of peace?

Far too often, in the People of God, authority has been exercised as a function giving rights over "subordinates." It has led to abuses of power. When it is identified with a temporal power, it no longer creates a community capable of being a leaven of communion; it gives rise to a human society, cohesive perhaps, but nothing more. Misunderstandings and tragic mistakes arise as soon as the office conferred upon men to animate the Church is identified either with monarchy or with some role in a civil society, albeit democratic.

Today however, authority can no longer be seen in terms of power, but only in terms of communion.

If authority is communion, then it is above all pastoral. It exer-cises vigilance to keep alive a sense of solidarity with the whole. It is possible, of course, to live the Gospel and have no organic link with the rest of the body. But at what cost! Freedom, so quickly confused with individualistic needs, leads to isolation. Each builds alone, in othe name of the purity of the Gospel, instead of remaining a ferment in the dough.

The centuries pass but this ministry of communion, entrusted to human beings, always remains the same: to address a living word, which penetrates down to the joints of the personality and inspires a change of direction. The propensity for revolt present in every human being hardly disposes us to listen to this word.

The question of a universal pastor demands much heart-searching. I would like to write more about it later.

(JOURNAL)

When Pope Paul VI took the first step by meeting Patriarch Athenagoras, he used his authority to set things in motion again. And when the same Paul VI addressed the Church of Constantinople as a sister-Church, with one word he brought ecclesiology out of a dead end.

The Bishop of Rome does not wait passively for others to act; he takes the initiative. If his authority were not recognized, his gestures would have no future.

I was present this morning at their third meeting: the reception of Patriarch Athenagoras in Saint Peter's.

Behind us sat a Greek woman, very agitated. She kept shouting out. She felt the seat she had been given was not appropriate to the dignity of her Church.

In front of us, a huge stage on which two identical armchairs were placed facing each other, one for the Pope, the other for the Patriarch. I am delighted that Paul VI intended in this way to have Athenagoras at his side. The Orthodox will appreciate this gesture.

Prayer first, then come the speeches. As the minutes pass, the silhouette of Paul VI seems to blend more and more into the shadow of the venerated patriarch.

Then a question arises. Supposing the idea of a two-headed Church were necessary for unity? But that would not be faithful to the image of the body. It would lead, as a result, to some sort of federalism.

* * *

The same question keeps coming up: with unity in mind, what would you like to see changed in both Protestantism and Catholicism?

Is it possible to answer without seeming holier-than-thou?

To see many Protestants give up intolerance, a form of alienation from Christianity. Protestantism has secreted the poison of intolerance to defend itself. One result is the need to segregate. The temptation to pull up the wheat with the tares leads to an unconscious, secret self-sufficiency. It ends up, strange as that may seem, in small-group triumphalism, as a Reformed pastor, a peaceful, kindly man, once said to me after a Protestant assembly.

As for Catholics, could we perhaps hope for many to liberate themselves from a need for power or even, at times for domination? This need is still ingrained in certain Church institutions. Far from stimulating creativity, it acts as a brake.

Overflowing with Hope

God Penetrates the Impenetrable

Beyond the immense open confrontation, the Church of tomorrow is coming into being. A springtime, at our door.

Every new birth is accomplished in patient suffering. But with the support of so many young Christians, how should we not be overflowing with hope?

Our hope is Christ within us. The more we allow ourselves to be penetrated by this reality, the firmer we can stand against wind and tide.

That is our hope. It keeps our heads above water, and comes to bring joy to our hearts the very moment doubts arise. It lets us see God, present despite the difficulties we have in believing whole-heartedly.

As the years pile up, vast areas underlying the personality make their presence felt more and more. For the most part they remain unknown. And yet it is from them that so many of our actions and so much of our behavior arise.

For too long, God was situated up in the attainable heights. But he is also the one who comes to live in our unfathomable depths. He is there, in our innermost being; he is our Heart of hearts.

(JOURNAL)

How many times have I called for the unity of the personality! By that I meant reconciliation of the self with God. But I am aware of the combat which must be waged daily, whatever our age. I can see the gaps in continuity, the roads that led nowhere. And I begin to wonder if it is not too pretentious to speak of attaining a unified personality.

It is granted for fleeting moments but, to be honest with myself, I have to admit that it is not a state I have attained once and for all. It is a direction, to be returned to tirelessly. The labor always has to be begun anew. Harmonizing opposites and turning them into complements.

If Paul had not written to the Christians of Thessalonica that their faith was making great progress,[17] I would be inclined to think that in this regard nobody has any hope of gaining ground.

When Paul asserts that love for others is increasing, however, I have no trouble seeing what he means. The more we advance, the more our sensitivity to others develops. Anyone who suffers from himself has such a capacity for understanding every human situation!

But is it true that our faith too makes progress? Does it become any easier when it has repeatedly been confirmed over many years? There are a great many situations where it is still found wanting.

Similarly, there are some events from which we never recover.

In 1962, to make it possible for a cooperative to start, we contributed our herd of cows, patiently bred by us over the years. The fact of giving up a possession was a relief.

But in the long run, we did feel the absence of farm animals. Life in the country loses part of its meaning if it does not involve intense participation in farm work. The herd more than anything else enabled us to follow the cycle of the seasons.

Gone that auspicious hour, repeated morning and evening—milking time! In the first years I was the only one to do the milking each day. No more calves being born! Helping the mother to drop her calf cannot leave anyone unmoved; it even has a certain solemnity.

Years have passed since our cows joined the collective farm. Our joy in that creation has not made up for the lack of full cowsheds close to the house.

* * *

Doubting God, and doubting God's forgiveness is one and the same thing. "He forgives, certainly, but some offences he can never forget...."

When doubt is in danger of overwhelming everything, darkness falls. All we can do is believe; there is nothing else left. The faith of the Church remains our one firm foundation. And that is not the business of a small élite of the pure and undefiled. It is lived by many, far more than meet the eye.

These people are not surprised at the many impulses arising from their depths. That is the stuff their humanity is made of. They are more surprised that they believe, in spite of everything, in a word that has been given. Not a set of logical conclusions but a simple word, spoken nineteen centuries ago. The storm has swept away before their eyes all that they had been clinging to. They are astonished to find themselves still standing upright on a bare rock.

Faith means believing without seeing. It is not afraid of the dark, nor of the dark regions of the personality. It is certainty. It allows us to go forward in spite of thick darkness.

In one sense, prayer is a step from doubt toward faith, a creative waiting to perceive in every event the Creator at work now. It is secret wonder and thankfulness for the gift of life.

(JOURNAL)
A friend asked, "Could all my life as a Christian be based on nothing but a gamble?"

My answer: We live surrounded by people who have given up the faith. With them in mind we can no longer express our faith in the language of bygone days. But our certainty, expressed in new language, is not founded on a gamble. It is based on the testimony of witnesses whose honesty is above suspicion.

As I said this, I was thinking of someone who is dear to me. He is active in trade unions and other such organizations. A skeptic by temperament, he told me one day how he had been visited by Christ: a living word heard in the silence of his heart when least expected! How could his faith—and mind in consequence—rest on a gamble?

* * *

It is no exaggeration to say that, in spite of a sincere profession of faith, large areas of our personality still remain in unbelief. Worrying about it gets us nowhere. Acceptance of the fact carries us forward.

Even if there are regions within us that remain obscure, God is able to penetrate all of them. He enters unbeknown to us. Little by little, he penetrates what is impenetrable.

When we accept the fact that nobody can attain faith in all its fullness, are we not calling faith itself into question? Not at all, if faith for us means the certainty that God is always invisibly present to the whole self, without, for all that, ever forcing us to total allegiance.

(JOURNAL)

If we assert that we have inner depths whose existence will remain almost entirely unknown to us, are we perhaps unwittingly endorsing psychoanalysis? I know little about that science, but I am still under the influence of a conversation I had with a leading figure in the field.

He feels that, far from being a cure-all, this science should be humble in coming to conclusions. Sometimes after analysis it is unable to achieve synthesis; treatment has only aggravated the inner anarchy.

If it is true that every human being is characterized by neurotic elements, in his opinion what counts in the long run is to turn the illnesses or neurotic conditions to good use. If, instead of stimulating creativity, they become destructive, then it is time to call on medical help. Psychoanalysis is a good remedy to apply when the others have failed.

He reminded me that throughout the ages intuition, under the name of "spiritual direction," has always been used effectively in the Church. It too is able to discern flaws in the personality into which the minimal foundations of the self collapse, causing serious disturbances. And these are not without their effects on the immediate social setting. In the long run they can contaminate.

He spoke of the doctors who are seriously affected in this way, but have themselves become psychoanalysts without subsequently undergoing the necessary regular check-ups. They change rapidly into the so-called wonder-workers of our time. They claim to possess the key to knowledge, when they only bring failures and ruin in their wake.

This doctor's modesty inspired complete confidence in analysis practiced seriously. He did not make a system out of it, or a philosophy.

How can we open the depths of our being to Christ and give him access to our personality? By telling him absolutely everything about ourselves. Showing him, in all candor, the blockages in our innermost life. And so, as the years go by, bringing to light buried values, which otherwise could never be used.

As we make our way forward, an answer comes. The dialogue goes on in spite of slackening or halting occasionally. One day, the core of the personality is reached. We surrender everything, irresistibly. Not only the inner contradictions, but even the people who condemn us or judge us have been confided to him.

Through the violence we have done to ourselves we discover a presence: Christ within us. Only the violent can seize. . . .

Refusing to hold on to anything equivocal is one way to a rebirth of the self. Whatever may be the value of this procedure, it has the advantage, when we are alone with God, of excluding any desire to play hide-and-seek with him.

The objection will be raised that "God sees everything anyway." Yes, but man constantly resorts to deviousness, as if he wanted to preserve a private domain for himself. This creates a kind of awkwardness in his relationship with God, as in a close friendship between two people, when one thinks he must conceal something the other obviously already knows.

Christ within us! We find that hard to accept, since guilt is such an all-pervasive part of the self.

Far too often the Jansenist attitude gets the upper hand: Lord, I am not worthy that you should come under my roof.[18]

Another within me! Finding him in prayer, the very moment when, apparently, I surrender mind and body to apprehend him.

Another within me! He uses my weakness and my inner contradictions. Even trials turn out to have a definite purpose: they leave us no other way out but himself alone. So there is beauty, even in trials.

(JOURNAL)

For a few days, some of the brothers and I have retired to a house with a terrace overlooking the sea.

What more could be desired! The air always stirring, the sea breeze, the scents, the bright light of morning and the cool evenings, after the heat and torpor of the day.

That is the time of day when I escape briefly to the western terrace, by the two orange trees.

Time for reflection. Tonight I realize how trying the past two years have been. So often I cannot see how I will be able to make the next efforts required, although I always do make them when the time comes. That is something I never experienced in my first twenty-five years at Taizé.

I am convinced of one thing: the immense combat to be waged is a challenge to the powers of a world of darkness. They do not want Christian unity. They know that Christ is in an agony of suffering at the sight of his people torn apart.

And so I have accepted that the combat could well become still more intense.

At peace once more, I now have only to master the fatigue this may well entail. Do everything possible to hold out on bad days. There is no other solution but to cast myself on Christ. Call upon him on every occasion, know that he is near.

This evening's meal shone with that. Nobody could have guessed, but I was a rich man, rich in the friendship of his brothers and of Christ.

What used to be known as "spiritual direction" also presupposes an attempt at total openness, but in the presence of another person.

Who could say of himself: there is nothing in me which has not been expressed, either in confession or to someone trustworthy?

Who can say: nothing is hidden, I know from experience this quality of transparence? It takes years and years to acquire this limpidity.

For anyone who renews this transparency day after day, times of peace come and, with them, such joy.

Shame at being alive, which clings in spite of everything, dissolves. According to the circumstances, it can take on different forms. It chokes all ability to communicate and destroys vital energies. It is fruitless suffering. Christian circles sometimes nourish this shame at being alive by their negative judgments. They often can awaken guilt feelings as no others can.

To be oneself, undisguised and guileless. Nothing falsifies communion and destroys the integrity of the personality more than wearing a mask.

When our being is transparent, failures, hindrances, and impossibilities are brought into new light.

Anguish, that source of powerful impulses, is itself absorbed. So often anguish can give rise to anger or love, callousness, or tenderness. Like a bank of fog that has to be crossed, anguish must be accepted rather than avoided or diverted. It brings with itself its own solution.

And the more we live in transparency, the more we become a source of peace for those around us.

(JOURNAL)

Every day brings a new combat. Every committed person knows that. Otherwise there can be no progress. But for all of us, the capacity to make decisions is constantly renewed, until the day we die. The energy of the will is continually being reborn; its resources are unsuspected and inexhaustible.

Often I review the lost opportunities, all the places where it might have been good to lay the foundations of the community, and I compare those localities with our Mâconnais, so poor in human qualities and, as for the Church, drained of vitality.

To live in the past or in the future is useless. Imagination only dramatizes things. Nobody can live without looking ahead to a certain extent, but anticipating is fatal.

Friendship, a Reflection of God's Face

The more we advance in self-awareness, the more we realize that we will die without knowing any more than the contours of our personality, which is afloat upon vast subterranean lakes. But rocks emerge from these waters, and upon them we can build.

One of these solid rocks is confidence placed in another human being.

When this confidence takes the form of friendship, a sense of security increases and a common endeavor becomes possible. Building together, not for oneself but for others, is the inevitable result.

Only when we know what it means to be alone with ourselves can we appreciate the value of certain encounters.

Through friendship we are able to glimpse an unseen world. There is no more luminous reflection of God's face on this earth.

Faith is not born of human friendship, but it does find support there. Through a series of friendships, going all the way back to the first community of Christians, so that what counts is not my faith, but the faith of the Church.

And so, from the very beginnings, this prayer has remained unchanged: "Look not upon my sins—my lack of faith—but on the faith of your Church."

(JOURNAL)

On the subject of friendship I wrote to one of my brothers: "Friendship is a value of unimaginable dimensions. Generally we only know its surface. It is only on rare occasions that we plumb its depths.

Through the dialogue and the serene openness it makes possible, we discover, oh not all, but a few components of our being. And so within us something new is created, perhaps a kind of birth in Christ."

In his turn, a brother wrote to me:

"In these times when God tests us to ascertain our degree of friendship with himself, our friendships with human beings and with our brothers take on a dimension of eternity."

Does not the burning thirst for relationships between human beings have its source in the presentiment of another and more essential communion, our relationship with Christ?

More than ever before, the younger generations are deeply interested in communicating. Are they not ripe to consider that, beyond the limitations of all human intimacy, at a given moment One alone can fill our solitude?

A close lifelong relationship is not granted to everybody. But a time of rare intimacy, an experience of friendship limited in duration, can leave its mark upon a whole lifetime. It wakens energies hitherto unknown. It transforms the core of the personality, making it more human and welcoming.

When anxiety regarding a friendship takes hold of a person, that can create in response emotional demands far out of proportion to the actual situation. This leads to constant disappointment which is the cause of inhibitions, refusals, and even revolt. We love for our own good, not unconditionally. There is no friendship in possessiveness. There is no friendship without purifying trials.

(JOURNAL)
Tonight, some of the young people asked me what it means to be gratuitous.

It is what someone does when he refuses to keep another human being captive.

This act involves a passover. A passing right over oneself, one might say in heroic language. This passover leads to a communion. Once achieved, it opens the way to new life as nothing else can.

And when friendship unites us with nonbelievers, we receive an additional benefit.

These days when people are becoming secularized and refuse our age-old Christian civilization, men and women who profess atheism sometimes generously desire encounter with Christians. Some of them have passed from anathema to dialogue. Yes, dialogue with them makes us more human.

Never as in recent years have I spoken so much with nonbelievers. Yesterday again one of them, a man of letters I have never met, sent me his latest book and wrote on the flyleaf: "Hoping that your open heart can welcome an agnostic."

And a few days ago, in the midst of the long series of meetings here, two young students from our region, neither of them baptized, came to tell me that they were soon to be married. They do not want a Church wedding. That would be dishonest, they said. The girl belongs to a family in which nobody has been baptized for generations, perhaps not since the French Revolution. The young man also comes from a non-Christian family. But the auspicious day of marriage should, they think, be made memorable by an event. Why not share a time together with both families present? So, on the evening of the wedding day I meet these two old Burgundian families in our Church.

Our conversation was simple. Dialogue was possible now because one man, Pope John XXIII, had made the breakthrough. That is what we told one another.

The bells stopped ringing. I went to my place, knowing that those unbaptized folk were still there, standing in the shadows throughout the evening prayer.

Peace: A Creation

We are scarcely aware that we have entered a new era, the nuclear age. To ensure the very survival of the human race, understanding among all people is essential. Will Christians be capable of promoting this process of communion among all, the creation of peace?

In this period of history, ethnic structures are breaking down. A partial and quite relative peace is not in the least due to mutual understanding, but to balance of terror. Nuclear weapons are capable of annihilating the entire globe.

(JOURNAL)

In these years when we are contemporaries of a long-drawn-out war, we were profoundly moved during prayer one night to hear a Vietnamese who was staying for a short time at Taizé say these words:

> *I am afraid of my fear,*
> *I am afraid of leaving you, Lord.*
> *I am afraid of my fear,*
> *I am afraid of not persevering to the end.*
> *Do not forget that I live for you.*
> *Give me the grace to give you my whole life,*
> *And the love to make me one with yourself.*

* * *

To prepare peace, should not our attention be focused on how to keep wars from happening?

Peace has to be prepared while there is still time, before the worst happens.

Some Christians are working at it with unparalleled generosity. But we are forced to recognize how difficult it is for them to stop conflicts, once begun.

Cooperating to bring about the progress and the liberation of all peoples, working for the advancement of all humankind means redressing a part of the injustice in the world and, at the same time, creating conditions that make for peace.

In order to take part in this creation of peace, many Christians in rich countries are working out for themselves a life-style suitable to this age of starvation. They give generously of their possessions. With the violence of peacemakers, they want to find concrete signs to awaken the conscience of Christians, and non-Christians as well.

But what can we do? Their gestures are signs, nothing more. They are anxious to put into practice what was asked of Christians fifteen centuries ago, when forms of capitalism were being initiated: "It is because some are attempting to take for themselves what belongs to all that quarrels and wars break out, as if nature were shocked that man puts division, by means of these cold words 'mine' and 'yours,' where God has put unity. . . . You are stewards of the goods of the poor, even when you possess them by honest labor or by inheritance."[19]

(JOURNAL)

Conversation with an economist. He is sure that the day is coming when the findings of the technological revolution will succeed in putting an end to starvation.

The tremendous responsibilities he has can be read in his face. This man stimulates the reflection that we are undertaking with others on how the poor countries can free themselves from the present situation.

Then we touched on the subject of reciprocity between continents.

The awareness of their status as human beings that the poorest have gained will make it possible for the indispensable complementarity between the peoples of the Northern and the Southern hemispheres to become a reality.

The perceptive powers of the peoples of the Southern hemisphere are astonishing. They apprehend the external world with an incomparable capacity for feeling and for intuition.

People of temperate or cold climates, on the other hand, use analysis to understand phenomena.

The creative and artistic capacities of the peoples of the Southern hemisphere represent an active force that could come to the rescue of the intellectual atrophy of Northern cultures. Any segregation of South from North means a slow death for the whole of humanity. The complementarity of cultures is the future awaiting us all. The interchange that will take place between the intuitive gifts of the one and the analytical gifts of the other is creative.

Will the West be able to compensate for its difficulty in entering into authentic human communion by opening itself to the spontaneity of Africans in particular? Will our individualism, reinforced as it is by an affluent civilization, learn by contact with the Southern nations how to share?

* * *

As a preparation for peace, the mixing of races also offers a solution to conflicts. A letter from one of my brothers in Brazil emphasizes one aspect of this:

> Life among people who are, together with those of India, the poorest in the world, has its times of fullness. The hardship of unemployment which afflicts us, since our European nationalities and culture arouse suspicion in the factories, is compensated by the hospitality we receive. A family is capable of giving to a foreigner all the food in their shack, and is prepared to go hungry for the next few days.
>
> Art in Brazil is flourishing, as a result of the mingling of races. The *"bossa nova"* in poetry, song and literature has an almost universal appeal. For the nations of the West it will be like the African contribution of jazz.

* * *

Would Christians be afraid of dirtying their hands by participating in the betterment of humanity and the creation of peace on earth? Pietism is to be feared when it prohibits all involvement in economics, politics and the social sciences. Doing the will of God does not consist simply in saying "Lord, Lord," but in making a courageous contribution to the common good.

In the years to come, one of the characteristics of genuine Christianity will be its ability to prepare new kinds of relationships among human beings. This will be political commitment in the broadest sense of the term: not partisan struggle, when horizons become narrower and when everyone runs the risk of serving the interests of a faction, but the building up of the city of man.

All of us are challenged by the necessity of sharing. This cannot be limited to a restricted area, to one local or national community. In a renewed awareness of the needs of people throughout the world, Christians will be required more and more to see themselves as members of humanity as a whole. That is the meaning of our vocation to catholicity, to universality.

To sustain this new thrust forward means coming to grips with multiple and contradictory interests. How can we avoid being trapped? How can we not get stuck in a quagmire alive with passions of every sort? Where can we place our foot without running the risk of being unable to withdraw it again? Yet on the other hand, how can we refuse to become involved?

Whether the new society is to be built with the Christians, or without them, is up to them. But at this point, tensions build up. Some, in their fanaticism, want to impose an exclusive solution, whereas there are complementary ways of being involved.

The violence of the disputes neutralizes generosity. Intolerance and the spirit of anathema among people deeply affected by the drama playing itself out before our eyes further cuts off those who were willing to collaborate. It is not unprofitable to recall that those who have suffered most in their past from intolerance sometimes become capable, in turn, of an intransigence comparable with that of the Inquisition.

Pluralism of approach is the only way to enter into the new tensions. For some, their particular genius would be to be a hidden presence among the world's poor. Others have the gift of taking part in vast practical initiatives. Still others are called to undertake well-thought-out reflection on ways of ending tyrannies. This whole spectrum is essential to the working out of peace among men.

(JOURNAL)

Conversation with a brother leaving Taizé to return to one of our fraternities. What will our life there be? A living word in the midst of injustice and segregation; a prayer, expressed by a way of life that is absurd in the light of reason; a language addressed to God, in all our actions among the most ill-treated; a page on which is being written the sufferings added for the sake of His body, which is the Church. [20]

Recently, a member of a religious order was protesting against the presence of one of our fraternities because our brothers refuse to commit themselves in exactly the same way as he does. The writer is an intellectual. He knows how to use his pen. He wants us in our turn to show where we stand by the pen. All we would have

*to do would be to sign a document and we would be committed
men. But committed to what, exactly?...*

*The fact of sharing day after day the sufferings of a monotonous
existence, of living under the same conditions as women and men
who have no hope, is a form of commitment that costs more than
signing petitions or writing manifestos, however justified they may
be.*

*I know that some manifestos have at times had shock value, and
have committed those who compromised themselves by signing
them. But the very least we can say is that nowadays there are more
than enough of them. So many people are canvassed to sign documents, to take sides for or against.*

*Isn't it more constructive to be people who listen? This attitude
has never hindered us from taking part in the life of others. For
those of my brothers who have lived or are living under the same
conditions as workers, for those who have plunged into the life of
the poorest of the poor, their very presence shows what they stand
for. No manifestos are needed. These sometimes do not commit us
in any way; they pacify our conscience, nothing more.*

*Working out praiseworthy resolutions at the close of a meeting
can lead to hypocrisy. We affirm in writing, we condemn, we ap-
peal, and it all changes our lives not one bit. This procedure is
rapidly becoming one of the diseases of the century.*

Creative Violence

Many young people, whether Christians or not, are trying to
revolutionize present-day structures by means of concrete actions.

For some, only violence can succeed.

Others are familiar with this saying from the Gospel: only the
violent take hold of the Kingdom of God; the lukewarm, the half-
asleep, the unthirsty exclude themselves. But these young people
know that Christ also said: happy the peacemakers.[21]

Violence of peacemakers! Could the whole spirit of the Gospel,
capable of bringing revolution on this earth, be condensed in this
apparent contradiction?

It is not a question of just any kind of violence. The kind that takes hold of the Kingdom is creative. It does not bear the stamp of a need for power.

In the name of Christ it is possible to set out on crusades of anger, to impose upon others partisan opinions, a sectarian spirit or some kind of purism. In the past, people have killed one another in his name. Some, by pen alone, have discredited other human beings. Destructive violence between Christians has devastated huge sectors of the Church of God.

Is not kindling destructive violence between Christians a means of crucifying the Body of Christ in the name of so-called noble motives? Far from taking hold of the Kingdom, is this not a way of making oneself unfit for it?

Since 1966, as a result of the large international gatherings of young people at Taizé, we could sense that the impatience of the young would soon explode, since too many older people were coldly rejecting all that was arising from the conscience of the young.

(JOURNAL)

(February 1968) Conversation with a group of young West Berliners. Of Protestant origin, they gave vent to their scepticism with regard to all Church institutions. Violence alone interests them. They have been deeply affected by the death of one of their friends. He was killed by a policeman during a demonstration.

They ask: Why does your community refuse to use the press to influence public opinion? You brothers are known in Germany and you could do a lot. Why do you, in your capacity as prior, not speak out more? I reply:

All the brothers are complementary, myself included.

Yes, but it's your job to speak. You don't know how much influence you could have.

What really matters is a man's inner self. The outward image some people might form is of little concern to me. And this inner man prefers a certain silence; he has very little faith in declarations.

You ought to write to the President of the United States.

I have done so, and I am under no illusions about the effect of my letter. Besides, many have intervened and the war is not over for all that.

So then violence is the only thing that pays.

Violence can only be the last resort, when all the means of passive resistance and persuasion have been exhausted. It is only possible to turn to that extremity when the mind has been purified of all personal interest. And we must never forget: "Whoever takes up the sword will perish by the sword."[22]

I urge them to read this very evening a suggestive text recently written on the "development of peoples." I stress the fact that, in this text, for the first time a Pope, after cautioning against the temptation to use violence, accepts in writing that it can break out in exceptional circumstances, "where there is manifest, long-standing tyranny which would do great damage to fundamental personal rights and dangerous harm to the common good of the country."[23]

Why have these young people come to question me? They are not interested in ecumenism. Protestant or Catholic matters little to them. They don't know where they stand with regard to their faith. We are all the more surprised to see them take communion at our daily Eucharist.

Back in the solitude of my room, I decide I cannot let them go home without listening to them once more. Violence can have a prophetic quality to it and so I dare not stop my ears. I recall that as he was dying, Jesus promised eternal life to a man of violence.

On their last morning, I invite them to breakfast at the house. I notice the look of steel on one girl's face, animated by a cold passion. She is forceful enough to create a kind of unanimity on the necessity of violence. If a psychiatrist had been present, he would have spoken of group psychosis. It is true that some of the prophets of Israel were far from being models of psychological balance! Fortunately these boys and girls, receiving explosive arguments full in the face just as I was myself, were able to rethink the issues with an impressive sincerity.

The Vietnam War is intolerable to them. They want to act. I reply: for my part I would like one of my brothers to leave for Vietnam with a young American who is in Taizé at the moment. This war has wounded him to the quick. And you, what can you do?

The girl who is spokesman for the group mentions Latin America. A revolution must be started there to liberate the poor. We must create more Vietnams, in Christian societies as well.

I answer that, perhaps, it is still possible to find solutions without bloodshed. Women and children are not asking to be killed.

For you, what counts is commitment. So finish your studies quickly, a minimum of education is indispensable as a foundation.

Once involved, perhaps some of you will, in good conscience, come to the point of rebellion against a manifest, long-standing tyranny that denies basic human rights and has no respect for life. At that point, you must still examine your own hearts. The temptation to violence is within us all, our whole lives long. If it leads to the conviction that we must destroy in order to rebuild, the most important thing is to question ourselves.

When you equate violence with destruction, are you not perhaps being fanatics of a single idea? Are some of you cherishing the secret hope of becoming political leaders and imposing your authority? The arguments may well be of the highest order, the real motives are not—neither selfless nor disinterested.

Destructive violence is in danger of escalating more and more. The moderates are killed off in the second or third wave, because they refuse to accept destruction as an end in itself.

It is true that in Latin America, our cross as Christians is the image projected by certain people who call themselves Christians. Contempt for the lives of the poor, the use of power, in other words violence in disguise—what an image of the Church! Newspapers and television do not fail to transmit the spectacle.

The need for power through money is one form of tyranny. It can also be exercised without money. There are police states in countries where capitalism is being undermined or has disappeared. And what powerful means of oppression are found there!

Tyranny can feed on the most humanitarian theories and, under the cloak of great ideas, conceal the worst kind of suppression of human rights.

* * *

Yesterday the Berliners. Today, although we are far out in the country and it is the dead of winter, I find I am still confronted by the same issues. Young people from another country ask me the same questions. From the very first moment I sense bitterness. There was none of that in the Berliners.

Their question, put briefly, was this: Why do you refuse to destroy Church institutions? You should set to work to sweep them all away. Without violence we will get nothing from the hierarchy. We would rather your community had never existed if it does not see things this way.

I try to understand. In the ensuing conversation, I remember saying to them: Do you know what your motivations are? Are you able to call your own motives into question? Do you ask yourselves about patience (patience means suffering), an essential ingredient in all creative work, in every rebirth?

The violence of peacemakers! It is creative violence, revolution-izing people and, by the challenge it presents, obliging them to take a stand. It has the power to communicate. It can be recognized by certain signs.

First, it is like a living protest in the face of hardened Christian consciences, which accommodate themselves to hatred or to injustice.

What a challenge when even one Christian becomes a living hope in the midst of a world of injustice, segregation, and starvation! Emptied of all hatred, his presence is constructive; it creates. This challenge is a blaze of love, it is a violence inhabited by a Presence. When someone's life is ablaze in this way, he kindles a fire on the earth.

(JOURNAL)

At Taizé, we have made use of violence in the face of a Christian conscience hardened by confessional separations and feeling quite comfortable with the divisions.

In our violence, contained to be sure, we looked for a language in which to shout out our indignation.

In the common prayer, in the singing of the Psalms, it found ex-pression and a way of being stimulated, incomparably.

Another sign of the violence of peacemakers: it is lifelong perse-verance in intimacy with another life, the life of the Risen Christ. If he finds us faithful until death, he rewards our perseverance with an intimacy which fills our being and transmits life.

Then we are granted the ability to discern beyond the world of things and events, beyond our transitory hopes, something much more intimate and much more profound. It is there that he awaits us. It is there that we meet him as we remain before him. It is there that he awaits us.

(JOURNAL)

Nearly three hours' conversation with a student, a revolutionary. He proposes a society based on justice, issuing from the spontane-ous impulses of man. For him a utopia has positive value; it is a creative force.

But at the same time, he makes the brutal assertion that the as-sassination of Martin Luther King was a good thing. The deed set vital energies free. For him, King was a hindrance to the de-liverance of mankind; he canalized the explosion of violence. Without him the summer could well be hot, destruction will be possible, and that will count in Europe.

I listen to him. His words make something bleed within me. At the same time I question myself. I ask myself what my own incon-sistencies and unsuspected prejudices are, when I see that the man I am talking to displays such blatant ones without realizing it.

Prophecy Is Not Dead

A hope is pulsing through the life of the People of God. Irrevers-ible events point to it. At times their diversity may be disconcert-ing, for this makes our tomorrow difficult to discern. But new life is flowing, and not just any kind of life.

No, prophecy is not dead.

Christians, divided for centuries, can no longer ignore one another. New generations of Christians can no longer bear to be separated when they go to encounter nonbelievers.

For these young people, God is not dead. What they violently reject is the fake dialogue and the clichés that emanate from some of their elders. But when their elders are able to express themselves in new language, they are understood as never before. Who will finally succeed in destroying the myth of a categorical rejection of the older generation? Many of the young have a need to refer to another's experience and, when it comes to that, age is irrelevant. It is easy for them to see that, if they insist on creating alone, they will achieve nothing.

For them, friendship is not a meaningless word. They see it in terms of sharing. Through them the People of God of tomorrow is being prepared: a great many groups are springing up in which the sense of common creation takes on an intensity never before known.

These little groups do not intend to become new institutions. They set a time limit for their duration in advance. They are capable of disbanding in order to preserve the provisional character of their situation. Many of them are concerned about the question posed by their existence: How to live in small groups without bringing about the fragmentation of the People of God and losing the sense of its universality?

(JOURNAL)
When I saw our church being built of concrete, a difficult time began for me. Now, years afterward, I cannot accept it any more readily. I wish it were almost completely underground, hardly visible to the eye.

Up till now, all of us have built with certain standards of the nonprovisional in mind. But the mobility of modern times makes us think seriously about a Church living as it were in tents.

This winter we destroyed the hard-and-fast elements within our church. Concrete did not stop us from making more flexible and movable arrangements. But there is still the exterior. What can be done? Hide it with trees?

We have learned a lot from the whole experience. Concrete brings with it rigidity and the impression of force.

Is not the primary demand made on Christians of our time to live as members of one family?

The spirit burst forth already in the early Church: they persevered, welcomed one another in their homes, shared meals, and the spirit of festival overflowed, irresistibly. In their work and in their difficulties, they shared everything in common. Nobody forced anyone else to be cast in the same mold; their unanimity found expression in a pluralism.[24]

They were not just any community, but a meeting of people in which he was present, the Risen Christ.

(JOURNAL)

A group of about forty young people question me. A girl's voice, fresh and timid, barely audible, says to me: the world of today is so complex; how can we, with our little bit of knowledge, play a part?

My reply: every woman and every man, whatever the extent of their knowledge, is granted one living truth, sometimes just a single word. Putting it into practice makes a person able to understand from within the various contemporary trends.

This truth brings us close to everybody—the peoples of China, Cuba, Eastern Europe, the United States—so that we can prepare crossroads where one day those who are now far apart will meet.

Back in my room, I continue the conversation in my mind.

Man is created for hope. For him all things are continually being made new.

One day, at the heart of our darkness, a living word lights up. Irresistibly, it opens the way to other people.

Christ does not force anyone to follow him.

The Gospel is not a system, a vice to hold fast other people's consciences and our own. The Gospel is communion.

In Christ, God made himself poor and obscure. A sign of God cannot be an image that overpowers. God does not ask us to work wonders beyond our means; he wants us simply to understand how to love our brothers.

In these years we can sense a new birth: the People of God moving toward communion.

Prophecy is not dead. Beyond the violence of the present, a young hope is arising.

Part Three

THE
WONDER OF
A LOVE

Come, the wonder of a love . . .
and may the wellsprings of jubilation
never run dry.

Journal: 4 September–20 October 1974

4 September

When I was young, at a time when Europe was torn apart by so many conflicts, I kept on asking myself: Why all these confrontations? Why do so many people, even Christians, condemn one another out of hand? And I wondered: is there, on this earth, a way of reaching complete understanding of others?

Then came a day—I can still remember the date, and I could describe the place: the subdued light of a late summer evening, darkness settling over the countryside—a day when I made a decision. I said to myself, if this way does exist, begin with yourself and resolve to understand every person fully. That day, I was certain the vow I had made was for life. It involved nothing less than returning again and again, my whole life long, to this irrevocable decision: seek to understand all, rather than to be understood.

5 September

With the opening of the Council of Youth a week ago, we leapt over a wall. Beforehand it seemed so high. We could have fallen back on the same side. Yet here we are, over it. A leap like that was not without a few scratches, of course. But on the very afternoon of the opening, my usual nap was peaceful, in spite of the fact that 40,000 young people were on the hill, and many Church leaders as well, for the most part overflowing with friendship, though some were reserved. Ahead lie other walls for us to leap over, other hills to climb. In the struggles to be waged, we will still manage to listen to the voices of children and the singing of birds, the ones brought by Paco from the Canary Islands for the opening day....

117

7 September
We have received piles of messages and telegrams. Clement has to answer them all. His is the merry laugh that so often lightens our fatigue; all at once he is slightly overwhelmed.

9 September
As a sign of the stage we have reached, we asked the young people to give up the small groups and special cells started four years ago. Perhaps we have not emphasized enough that this was in order to create new signs: small provisonal communities that spring up everywhere, communities that see themselves as part of the Church, in solidarity with the People of God and with a local identity. It would be too easy for them to act in the name of the Council of Youth or of Taizé. That would mean unconsciously involving themselves in forming a movement or even, ultimately, one more Church.

Several times in the past people urged us to start a new Church. Such an undertaking would have given the lie to our quest for reconciliation. It would have meant entering into an age-old process that has rent the Body of Christ in the past. We have suffered too much from that process to make use of it ourselves. Those who have set out to create a new Church have often experienced extraordinary enthusiasm at the outset, but in time the usual failings cropped up once more.

10 September
Remarked last night to Hassan: your presence here guarantees that soon we shall be unable to speak of the love of God without discovering the treasures of trust in Him found in the tradition of your fathers, Islam.

14 September
Dramatic arrival of a group of young Vietnamese. A girl told everybody in church: "It's the first time we've been in a country at peace where we can listen to the birds and talk freely, with no

whistling of rockets, no bombings, no sleepless nights spent looking for shelter in the trenches.''

18 September
The discovery of a secularized world makes us hesitant to express what could distinguish us, as Christians, from the rest of mankind. It is true that, in the heart of God, the Body of Christ is as vast as humanity, and the thought that even one human being could be excluded seems incredible.

21 September
Days made memorable by departures for distant lands. In one week, the same words spoken three times over to those who were leaving us: you are going to find tyranny, executions, killings; in the presence of Christ, cry over your nation; let us pray together for that beloved country.

2 October
Before he left to return to Africa, a boy from the Congo told us about the death of his friend Jonas. Last May, he had set out with others for a meeting in a village as part of the preparation of the Council of Youth. A boat had an accident and Jonas was drowned. Some felt he had been murdered for political motives. His parents declared that "he died for God." Tonight we celebrated a Eucharist in communion with Jonas. When he was alive we could say to him, "Pray for us." More than ever now it is possible to keep on saying the same words to him. . . .

8 October
The stakes of what we have begun must be high indeed, to bring with them trials I cannot allow to show for fear of discouraging even the most stalwart.

11 October
Vienna. Invited by Cardinal Koenig to the closing of the Austrian Church Synod. I found him the same man who used to come to eat

with us in our flat in Rome during the Vatican Council. In him we can already sense what openness to everybody means; he is a man who shows what the Church is going to become.

The prospect of speaking in his cathedral from a raised choir, which makes one feel so isolated, aroused some apprehension. The fear vanished as soon as we entered that place of prayer together and paused before a glorious figure of motherhood—a venerable painting of the Virgin Mary, hanging on a column.

12 October

Absolutely spontaneous meeting with some young Austrians. We were packed tightly together, too many for the restricted space of a Baroque church in Vienna, yet we managed to communicate. They had drawn up a list of questions, all dealing with current concerns, some of them blunt, like this one: "How not to be put off by Church institutions?"

Yes, the institutions can alienate us, brand us indelibly, sometimes cause deep humiliation. But we can also alienate ourselves, by fighting against them. Christ never calls us to crusade against anyone. He does not ask us to use our energies to abolish but to fulfil. He himself did not abolish the fossilized institutions he faced, those of the old law; he strove to fulfil them.

Creating communion with Christians who wound us does not mean compromising, of course. Love is not blind.

13 October

Frankfurt. Speaking in public in Germany for the first time, I have a vivid memory of a young German prisoner, who died quite close to Taizé in the winter of 1945-46.

In 1940 when I settled in Taizé alone, it was, of course, to prepare a place where a parable of communion could be lived. But it was also to give shelter then and there to political refugees, especially Jews. I was in Switzerland helping someone to cross the frontier when, in November 1942, the Gestapo broke into the house at Taizé and I was compelled to stay away for almost two years. In

1945 the situation was reversed, and camps for German prisoners were set up in our locality. I was allowed to invite some of these prisoners to the house every Sunday morning, for a short time of prayer and to share with them the food that was so hard to come by. Poverty was our common lot. Among those who came Sunday after Sunday, a young Catholic priest stood out. His whole being shone with serenity.

It was a time when, more than ever, hatred produced hatred. One day, some local women whose husbands had been deported to Germany and killed in concentration camps, in an act of strange desperation, attacked one of the prisoners. The one they fell upon was none other than this young German priest. In his weakened state, it meant death for him. During his last hours, there was nothing in his heart but peace and forgiveness. I saw what I had known for months: he was a reflection of God's holiness, in the fullest sense of that word.

In Frankfurt, I told this story. And as modern technology made it possible for me to be heard simultaneously in both Germanies, I told my listeners that any of them who had tragically lost a father, brother, or husband could contemplate him in the face of that young priest.

20 October
With the young brothers, the Eucharist is celebrated in the house, near the Coptic icon showing Christ with his hand on his friend's shoulder. We remain kneeling there for a long time.

Last Friday, after a similar celebration, we were asking one another how our vocations had come about. We all agreed that the origin of a vocation was surrounded by ambiguities. But some could see the starting point in a kind of visitation, an annunciation, confirmed as time went on. The words "annunciation" or "visitation" came so spontaneously to their lips. Men of the previous generation would have repressed such words. At that age they would have been wary of putting into words the unique experience of one who aspires to follow Christ.

You Aspire to Follow Christ

You aspire to follow the Risen Christ: how can you know that you have encountered him?

Rather than trying to feel his presence, will you be able to discern God in the simple events of life, and put into practice every day the suggestions he places in you?

What is the sign that you have encountered Christ? When you are led, irresistibly, to leave everything behind, to leave yourself behind, not knowing where you are heading. You have encountered him when, try as you may to stop your ears, within you his words ring out: "You, come and follow me."

Already long before Christ's coming, a believer of the Old Testament wrote: "You who wish to serve the Lord, prepare yourself for trials. Be transparent of heart and steadfast." (Sirach 2.1f).

All or Nothing

Choosing Christ is a matter of all or nothing; there is no middle ground. Will you go to the point of bearing in your body the marks of Jesus and the burning of his love? They become visible in you when you are able to tell him: "You loved me first. You are my joy, my essential love—may that be enough for me."

If you wish to follow him to the very end, no matter what the cost, prepare yourself, in the poverty of your life, to know times of struggle: the fidelities of daily life which, through simple, ordinary acts, link you to an immense reality. And in you is formed a humanity permeated with understanding for everyone, a heart wide as the world.

By what other sign can you recognize that you have encountered the Risen Lord? When the inner struggles you wage in order to follow him, the trials that can even cause floods of tears to flow within, when this whole combat, far from making you hard and bitter, is transfigured and becomes a source of new energy.

Such a transfiguration is the beginning of the resurrection, already here on earth. It is an inner revolution, the passover with Jesus, a continual passing from death to life.

In this inner revolution, all that could devastate your being—loneliness, loss of meaning, feelings of uselessness—everything that otherwise would shatter the fibers of your soul, all these things no longer block the way forward, but instead lead to a breakthrough from anguish to confident trust, from resignation to creative enthusiasm.

You aspire to follow the Lord, so do not be afraid of entering a passover with Christ. If you do not stop your ears when you hear him say "Come, follow me," you will be surprised to find yourself answering:

> I have recognized you, and so I want to stay close beside you as you listen to the simple words I stammer in prayer—you, the Christ of glory, risen within all who are searching for you. I also want to be able to accompany you in your agony for mankind, since you stay close beside anyone who is in distress, anyone who is struggling on behalf of many others. To put my trust in you, to acquire a steadfast heart, I will go to the point of gathering up all my energies and, violently if need be, go so far as to anchor my heart to God's heart, for I have understood: only the violent take hold of the realities of the Kingdom of heaven.

A life based solely on the confidence he places in us is love at its purest, not an illusory love which is content with words, but trusting that flows from a love that constantly takes hold of the whole being, a love strong as death.

The Risk of Living

You aspire to follow Christ: you can only encounter him by placing your trust in him; there is no other way.

But how can you trust him and follow him in a lifelong commitment when you are so afraid of making a mistake or, later on, of having made a mistake?

To prepare yourself to say this yes, and then to live it, you need to have someone to talk to about yourself. And not just anybody. Otherwise you would look for someone who follows your line of least resistance, and you will never become a creator that way. You can speak about what lies buried in your heart only to someone who has the gift of discernment and is experienced, who can read what lies beneath the contradictions of the personality.

The person who exercises this ministry has no method, no theory. He does not give the same answer to everyone—it all depends on each one's basic gift.

To one person he will have to say: "Leave everything, right away; otherwise you would be running away from God." To someone else, just as eager to follow Christ, he will say instead: "To commit your whole life to God, first gain the necessary qualifications in a profession, to prepare yourself to serve others. Interrupting your professional training now would be taking the easy way out."

To all, in any case, he will express this certainty: "You will only know God by taking the risk to live from him, in a life that is exposed, not protected or withdrawn. And not just for a while but for your entire lifetime. Dare to take this risk over and over again."

The fear of making a mistake is present in youth but it can also return much later. Some people begin to flame in their middle years, thinking they have finally discovered the love of their life. They emphasize the errors that surrounded the decision they made when they were young, forgetting that no action on this earth is absolutely pure; if so we would be angels.

When the yes to Christ has been confirmed by the person who has known how to listen to you, go ahead. If you remain in the quagmire of hesitations or regrets, you are wasting your time, time that no longer belongs to you—it is God's now. The portion of error or ambiguity that surrounds every decision will be consumed by the fire of God's Spirit.

You aspire to live dangerously for the sake of Christ, and so every day you will ask yourself the meaning of his words: "Whoever wants to save his life will lose it." And one day, you will understand what this absolute means.

How will you come to understand? Search. Seek and you will find.

PRAYER

Agreeing to lose everything for you, O Christ,
in order to take hold of you
as you have already taken hold of us,
means abandoning ourselves to the living God
and praying with you: "Father, not what I want,
but what you want."
Losing everything in order to live from you,
O Christ, means daring to choose:
leaving ourselves behind to walk no more
on two roads at once.
. . . saying no to all that keeps us
from following in your footsteps,
and yes to all that brings us closer to you
and, through you, to those you entrust to us.
For anyone who chooses the absolute of your call
there is no middle ground.
Following you, being women and men of communion,
means coming nearer and nearer
to an unseen martyrdom—
bearing in our bodies the agony of Jesus
and so becoming signs of the radiance of God.

Journal: 10 November 1974–20 March 1975

10 November
On this Sunday afternoon, in Notre Dame, Paris, the wish was expressed that I should speak as I do every week in Taizé—saying a few words about the Gospel, giving news, and dealing with the most urgent questions in the hearts of the young. But here in this venerable cathedral, everything is different. When I was a boy we used to listen as a family, with our earphones on, to the Lenten talks broadcast from Notre Dame. Father Samson's voice was like the prophet's reaching us high up in the Jura Mountains. I am astounded to find myself, a man with no talent for oratory, speaking in the same place.

Besides, there is no simultaneous translation. At Taizé, that makes it possible to be heard in several languages at the same time, which simplifies everything. I am in the habit of telling my brothers who are interpreting in their booths: translate just as you want to; say something else if you think it best; it doesn't matter in the least. Then everything is easier.

As we left, some people were distributing leaflets. When we come across this kind of extreme pronouncement, we should at least be glad that the authors have had this chance to vent their bitterness.

11 November
Yesterday in Notre Dame I quoted the African who, just before he left for home, was worried: "In the days immediately before the opening of the Council of Youth, I wondered if the *First Letter to the People of God* we were working on would be understood, if its strong language and its basic intention were going to be comprehended. The day it was read out I was relieved; the young people had realized that it was not mainly about ourselves but about the Body of Christ, the Church, called to be a worldwide community of sharing. Our intention had got across; we were not making a destructive analysis, but expressing demands that can only be made of those we love."

There are some who find it hard to understand that we associated ourselves with the text of that letter to the People of God. In its sometimes vigorous expressions they did not recognize Taizé's usual way of speaking, as if we had somehow left the beaten track.

It is true that tone often counts more than content, and that it would be possible to see that letter as a premature pronouncement from on high. Those who wrote it, however, wanted nothing more than to put into practice the Song of the Virgin Mary, when she calls for greater unity among men, when she says that, by the coming of her Son, "the powerful will be humbled and the poor raised up." The letter draws directly upon that woman's words. Why does the intuition of the Virgin Mary, expressed in the language of today, upset certain older people?

The young African was right. The *Letter to the People of God* can only be understood in its context. It was written by young people who, for four and a half years now, have been constantly returning to the starting point, the threefold celebration of the Risen Christ. Since Easter 1970 they have been meditating on these words: "We celebrate the Risen Christ in the Eucharist . . . we celebrate him by our love for the Church . . . we celebrate him in our brothers and sisters. . . ."

21 November

Letter from some political prisoners in Chile: "On the 30th of August, in prison, we celebrated a Mass to ask that the opening of the Council of Youth go well. We have just finished arranging a little chapel in the prison; it will be a place for worshipping Our Lord."

23 November

Many are finding it difficult to stand an autumn wetter than any in living memory. And yet it is possible these days to turn one's attention within. The oak log in the fireplace gives off little explosions. Under the eaves there is a pile of twigs for feeding the fire; their local name is "charbonnettes." Without them the flames would die down; the log would smoulder and give no heat.

The last ten years pass before my eyes, in particular the growing numbers of young people coming up to this place of prayer. When our Church of Reconciliation was built in 1962, its huge dimensions were hard to accept. And now it is often too small.

So many conversations suggest that the desertion of the churches by the young will continue to increase. Little communities spring up, but seldom do they manage to last, to the point that the uncompromising words of Christ come to mind: "When the Son of Man comes, will there still be faith on earth?" There is no answer except to continue with the young people, some of whom cover enormous distances, even in winter, to come here. At the moment there are some from Australia, Finland, and Norway.

27 November

Francisco has just lost his young wife. She was only twenty-five. There was a car crash involving all the family except himself. In the ambulance she was just able to say to him and to his son Martinho; "I love you." These Portuguese immigrants, who live in the village, are such close friends of ours. We go to see him; I sit on his right, Daniel on his left. From time to time it is obvious that his heart is broken. He can only lay his head on my shoulder, sobbing helplessly. Several times he says, "Our God directs all things." He knows that his two children are out of danger. He is going to live for them: "I will be everything for them; I will always stay with them."

On Sunday morning, a few hours before the accident, little Martinho happened to be beside me at the Eucharist, and together we went among the people bringing the peace of Christ. As always he was dancing and hopping along, with the happpiness of a child who is loved. He would learn of his mother's death on leaving the hospital. What a burden this child of six will have to bear now! Unlike an adult, he cannot see things in perspective. He will know in his own flesh the meaning of the words from the Second Vatican Council that have remained with me more than any others: "Man is sacred by the wounded innocence of his childhood."

28 November
In general we bring our deepest humiliations on ourselves. Why wear ourselves out looking for their cause elsewhere?

30 November
Leaving for Rome, as every year at this time. Yesterday evening, conversation with Jean-Pierre. He himself is surprised at what he said the other evening when we were all together. It was something he had never before put into words. That evening, he spoke of his happiness. And yet, for years his work has been monotonous and exacting: answering the telephone while typing out letters and texts. All that labor is not child's play. I often hesitate to ask him to type revisions of the same text several times over. But Jean-Pierre assures me that for him, his work is part of a whole where everything has its place. The secret of his happiness? He does no more than hint at it: the certainty of a presence.

2 December
Fatigue surfaces as usual at the beginning of a stay in Rome, after a long period of work in Taizé. Joyful walk across the Piazza Venezia. Up to the Capitol for the panorama of the city. After Mass at the *Gesù*, we remained in the huge empty church, going from one spot to another. A crib has been put out for the Christmas season. Churches are lovely when they make you feel at home, and you can come and go as you please.

3 December
Welcomed Enzo and his wife. Not so very long ago, his features showed the weariness of a boy who had to rise very early in the morning to help his parents clean offices. Today he is a young scientist, engaged in nuclear research. With his team he has just succeeded in isolating a particle. He has been working intensely, and his transparent face shows the effects of lack of sleep. His voice is hoarser than usual. Sofia and he talk about the young Italian Christians; they see them exploding into many little groups and

trends, which cannot possibly come together. They are extremely worried.

8 December
Max went to the Piazza di Spagna for the prayer in the open, which takes place every year on this day. The Pope noticed him and told him he would like to see me.

Even if the weight of Roman institutions could be crushing for anyone who let himself succumb to discouragement, coming here every year in December is still essential. Peter died in Rome. Christ entrusted to him a definite charge in the Church. It is for us, by our burning confidence in him, to help the Bishop of Rome to divest himself of enormous structures so that his ministry becomes more and more that of a universal pastor, exercising for all Christians an ecumenical pastoral vocation and leading the Church to become a ferment of communion throughout humanity.

9 December
Why are Christian youth movements disappearing? Many young people like to meet together to deepen their understanding of the Gospel, to pray and to look for commitments in society. But organized movements hold little interest for them. What new means can we find with them of rooting their lives in Christ and in the essential of his message?

14 December
Return to Taizé. Once again the Bois Clair looms ahead, overhung by a long black cloud—a narrow tunnel that has to be gone through in order to reach home. The choice of the village of Taizé remains a mystery. Why, at the beginning, did I not stop fifteen kilometers further on, among the open hills overlooking the plains of the Saône?

22 December
A brother hands me a page of a letter to read over. It came several months ago from a Young Christian Worker:

"To link us with the ecumenicity in which I profoundly believe and which strikes me every time I come to Taizé, speak, Brother Roger, for the young workers. Many of them are looking to Taizé. I am going to bring some fellows from the factory to the opening of the Council of Youth; that will lift our action into the dimension of the universal. But speak, brother, speak for the others."

Speak! But what can one man's words do? All together, yes, we can speak. Four and a half years ago, when we announced the Council of Youth, it was already the same question: what can one man do alone? What can a few brothers do? Not much. But together, with a clear vision of the People of God, we shall live a life we never dared hope for.

29 December

In the plane, with Robert, on the way to Latin America. Before the opening of the Council of Youth, powerful suggestions had been made. I had been asked to go to places where things are critical, alone or with young people, depending on the situation. The country where a visit seemed most necessary this year is Chile. To go there to listen, pray, and try to understand the poor and all who are giving their lives.

In our luggage is the episcopal ring that belonged to Bishop Larrain. At the end of the first session of the Second Vatican Council, when he was returning to his own country, that Chilean bishop slipped off his ring at the airport and said to a friend, "Take this to Roger, as a token of my faithfulness in the ecumenical vocation." Misunderstood throughout his lifetime, that man had to deal with the most incredible cross-currents imaginable as he worked to create a new awareness among Chilean Christians. He was also one of the founders of the Latin American Bishop's Conference. If he had not died in an accident, he is the one we would be going to visit first. Since we never keep anything of value in our house, his ring will be passed on to his successor, the present Bishop of Talca.

31 December
Short stop in Mexico for a gathering of young people from this country and all the countries of Central America, in a poor district of the city of Guadalajara. We did not come here in order to run a meeting; we are making a visit to discover in human faces reflections of the face of God.

1 January
Today the Holy Year begins. The organizers in Rome wrote to ask me to send a message for the young people. Before leaving for Latin America, I wrote them the following words:

"Originally a jubilee was the announcement of a year of celebration. Could this year of reconciliation be a celebration of forgiveness? You are members of the youngest generation of Christians: will you be able to help your elders to make it the year of peace? In every reconciliation, in every communion restored, new vitality and a new springtime come into being. This springtime will mean the end of our mutual condemnations, the old ones and the new ones. And in our turn we will be bearers of friendship and reconciliation for those around us, creators of peace among men, including those who do not share the faith of Christians."

2 January
Warm welcome at Santiago. The cardinal is at the airport.

A simple journey like ours answers people's longing to be visited in the dark periods of life.

3 January
This morning we were shown our program, planned out hour by hour. At the top of the list, a meeting with General Pinochet. With the situation as it is, seeing him is out of the question.

Out of all the many meetings today, one conversation with a few young people is going to remain with me. The word "Church" constantly recurred on their lips. They had had many reservations about it before, but they now see the Church of Chile becoming just what they were hoping for: a place where everyone is listened to, a house where nonbelievers are brothers and sisters of believers. At the end of our meeting one of them, who knows what it means to commit one's life to the cause of justice and who has gone through agonizing ordeals, summed up what really mattered for them: "To live out a radical commitment to the Gospel in a situation which, humanly speaking, is hopeless, we are seeking to be the salt hidden in the earth."

4 January
The Committee for Peace plays a unique role in this country. It is composed of about a hundred people who give themselves unsparingly, visiting those in difficulty, helping prisoners and people under arrest, and feeding undernourished children. At their head, a young priest who has been to Taizé, Christian Precht. He is constantly on the breach.

5 January
Visit to a base community in a poor district. We pray with them. A young couple puts us up for the night in their shack. We all sleep in the same room, with the four children, our beds separated from theirs by a few pieces of wood. One of the children has an earache and cries all night long. Through the slits in the planks, cold blasts blow in from the Andes. The dogs howl for hours on end. A night of waiting. A vigil.

6 January
The most impressive meeting of this visit to Chile—with Madame Luis Corvalan. She is of Indian blood. At fifty she seems so very young. Her husband is in prison, her eldest son has been tortured.

Until we met today, Madame Corvalan had not understood how it came about that Pope Paul VI had intervened one night and prevented her husband's execution. She did not know that we telephoned from Taizé to Rome that night to ask the Pope to intervene at once.

At the end of our conversation this woman, wife of a Communist leader, said, "Do tell people in your country that there are Christians here who are a light." She herself is probably not a believer. As she was leaving, she asked if she could come back in the evening with other wives of political leaders in the previous government. She also spoke of their tortured children.

"Salt of the earth," the young man said the other day. "Light for others," said Madame Corvalan today. The very same paradox as in the Gospel. Hidden salt at the side of the oppressed, with no obvious effect, but at the same time the light of the world, bearers of an enlightening word or a liberating action.

13 January

Back in Taizé. Martinho comes to see me regularly after school. He knocks at the glass-paneled door and comes in with quick, light steps. Two months ago, he would have told a story straight out of his imagination in a loud voice. Since his mother's death he enters without a word, silently gives me a kiss, pulls up a stool and stays a moment or two, resting against me. If I am talking to someone, he looks as if he doesn't see them, even if they know each other well. He, the fearless one, lowers his eyes as if staring into a void. The void is there: a mother, the most caring of mothers, has disappeared.

25 January

From Latin America, the Council of Youth seemed to me like a slight breeze bearing along a few seeds of communion. A breeze carries, without being visible in itself.

All communion is both strong and fragile at the same time. It is strong when, even unknown to us, part of the robe of Christ, that robe which is the Church, is being woven, with many and varied threads: some bright and joyful, others dark with human blood.

But we also know that communion is something fragile—we here on the hill are people who have never wanted to create a movement or attract a following.

8 February
Letter from one of our brothers living in Bangladesh. The need there is considerable. He reports these words of a young Bangladeshi: "If you have come here to add one more project to all those that have already been brought from the West, go back home. But as you have come first and foremost to pray, go and get all your other brothers and bring them too."

22 February
At our yearly council meeting, we looked for a gratuitous sign to live out that would point the way to love of the Church. The only answer is the call to holiness. The distinctive feature of this call is a joy which does not come from ourselves; an Other clothes us in it. Is it difficult to discern the presence of that Other? Sometimes we call him the Stranger. And yet he is there all the time, now in light, now in shadow. It is we who are far away, we who are loath to live the combat of the light. This combat is real! That of watchman in the night. Will we be those watchmen in the night of the Church?

27 February
When I leap out of bed, a surprise: trees and fields bathed in midsummer light. Two sparrows have settled in the nesting-box nailed to a branch of the lime tree. They come and go, disappearing into the dark hole where their brood awaits them. At the window you only need to lift your eyes at any moment to notice birds, just now the blue-tit with its pale yellow breast.

28 February
Invited to speak in the cathedral of Saint Pierre, Geneva. How could I not think back to the time, more than thirty-two years ago,

when we used to go every morning to pray in this very church with young people? After the first two years in Taizé, when we had to flee from the Gestapo, Geneva became our place of refuge.

6 March
For the first time Alain tells me the words he has repeated to himself over and over again for many years: "Jesus my joy, my hope, my life."

17 March
Conversation with Angelina on abandonment in God. It is when we are being buffeted on all sides that we get up again most quickly: one blow counteracts the effect of the previous one, one difficulty drives out another. Leave the worries that haunt you till later. It is true that what some write about us cannot leave us indifferent. A visit from the writer of the most cutting remarks revealed all the makings of an inquisitor. He is one of those who batten on the spoils of others.

20 March
Reread the letter written to me, four months before he died, by a psychiatrist whose reputation had spread far beyond the borders of his own land. He already knew how serious his illness was: "For some time now cancer has lost its hostile, alarming character. It has the role of a loyal collaborator, a kind of stimulus helping to change many things in me, stirring up, challenging, and opening up new and vast perspectives."

In this man prayer and action were one. In the little spiritual testament he left behind, he reflects on the possibility of turning human weaknesses to advantage. He admits that for a long time he suffered from a sense of his limitations. "Then came the time when I realized that the very acceptance of this feeling of insufficiency and limitation could bear fruit. I must not look at what others are doing or at their abilities, but rather recognize my limitations and fully accept them. That is the source of liberation; and then, I have no need to compare myself with others or look at their abilities. The feeling of inferiority and the impression of being excluded have contributed enormously to my growth as a human being. They have given me access to myself and this is so important for my patients: not only to be able to accept them with their fears and their weaknesses, that goes without saying, but even more, to know that those fears and weaknesses have their positive side, that they can lead to something good."

Fragile as Vessels of Clay

There is one thing we shall never fully understand: why has God chosen us, fragile vessels of clay, to transmit a part of the mystery of Christ? And why do some respond to this call and others not at all?

"It is in vessels of clay that we carry this treasure, the Risen Lord," wrote a witness to Christ nearly two thousand years ago, "to make clear that the radiance comes from God and not from us. We are hard pressed on all sides, but not crushed; we are brought down, but not destroyed. Always and everywhere we carry about in our bodies the agony of Jesus, so that in our bodies the life of Jesus may also be revealed." (2 Corinthians 4: 7-10).

Reveal and transmit Christ! By the lives we lead be a reflection of the Risen Lord! And yet we know him so little. If we had only our weak faith or our personal qualities to count upon, where would God's radiance be? It is not for nothing that God chose to reveal himself through our human frailties. How easy it is for us to make our own a prayer of Christians of the early Church. They too loved Christ without ever having seen him, and they said to him: "You do not look on our sins, but only on the faith of your Church."

Those who agree to transmit by their lives a part of the mystery of Christ, those who trust him even in the deserts of their lives, know that their choice can bring them closer and closer to unseen martyrdom. But for them, no matter what happens, no failures are ever final: hard pressed on all sides, they are not crushed; brought down, they are not destroyed.

All who live out to the utmost the consequences of Christ's call see their hearts opening to the universal: refusing to spare themselves, they become capable of understanding everything in others, of sharing their pain and their distress. Far from becoming hardened, far from becoming inured to suffering, as the years pass their hearts become all-encompassing.

Although everything seems to conspire to make them give up, although they carry within themselves the agony of Jesus, which is the suffering of people all over the world, how is it that they are not overwhelmed and exhausted? Their secret is this: at every moment, they commit everything to Christ—other people's troubles, their own trials, all that assails them. Without a prayer for their enemies as well, a part of themselves would settle into darkness.

As we continually commit everything to God, we learn to cast all upon him, even our tired bodies. And then everything comes to life, to the point that the Risen Christ reveals himself in our very bodies. With our bodies we sing to him. All that is within us begins to sing again, until we are filled to overflowing, "Jubilate Deo, jubilate Deo."

PRAYER

O Christ,
you offer us a Gospel treaure;
you place in us a unique gift—
the gift of bearing your life.
But, to make it clear
that the radiance comes from you
and not from us,
you have placed this incomparable gift
in vessels of clay,
in hearts which are poor.
You come to make your home
in the frailty of our beings,
there and nowhere else.
In this way, we know not how,
you make us, poor and vulnerable as we are,

the radiance of your presence
for those around us.

Journal: 29 March–19 September 1975

29 March
The Eve of Easter. After two months of an early spring (never in living memory has the like been known), icy cold grips us. The young people who have come for Holy Week are floundering in the mud. At night, in the church, some fall asleep on their knees, in prayer.

In Dahomey, a young African priest, Alphonse Quenum, and six other persons were recently condemned to death on political grounds. Sent this telegram to the President of the Republic of Dahomey: "With thousands of young people gathered at Taizé we learn of the seven death sentences including that of Father Quenum. In the name of human dignity pardon them. Do not wound the conscience of the young."

30 March
Easter morning. Meditation on perseverance. Loving to the very end does not come naturally: there are dead ends and failures. And the inner tug-of-war starts up. He is at it, the tempter; he tempted Christ, and to us he whispers, "Give up persevering!" And at times he insinuates, "You know, other loves will refresh your loving," Go right through dead ends and failures, don't avoid them or by-pass them; pass from one stage to another stage. Anyone who perseveres in giving his whole life gradually discovers, at every turn, another life welling up: the Risen Christ.

9 April
Letter from our brothers Michel and Bruno. Enough to keep me singing all day. Bruno tells of the Brazilian shanty-town where he works. "I could not keep going were it not for your letters...."

And Michel: "In Paraguay among the poor peasants, I spent an austere Holy Week. Perhaps it was not so bad, it gave me the chance to come to terms with the difficulty I had in leaving Taizé again. Five weeks in the community, surrounded by the warmth of our brothers, was enough to make Latin America seem very empty at first. But I am discovering too that our life with a few brothers in Brazil is authentic enough to keep on stimulating us."

12 April

In the spiritual wasteland of present-day Europe, how can we point to the only way out of the darkness and the fog? For at least a century now, the old world of Europe has been slowly sinking into an ocean of scepticism or indifference; what parable can we offer to lead people to draw their life from God? A few years ago, Europe seemed to be in a prerevolutionary state. Today that revolution bears the names pessimism, despair, nihilism, and introspection.

18 April

Yesterday evening, took a walk in the meadow, westward. Gusts of cold wind blew from the north. The clear sky promised a night of frost. Near their shed the sheep born this year were beginning the dance which, every evening for two months, they do at the same place. In the distance, a small grey patch on the grass. I found a little lamb lying on its side. I carried it away, its head resting on my arm. It had the look of the newly born. When I took it to the shed it seemed too weak to be interested in the milk bottle. Then, as it gradually warmed up, it began to suck. This morning I hurried to visit it: had it survived the night? It was there, wiggling its tail at the sound of my voice.

19 April

Conversation with Eric's father. In spite of his seventy-eight years, this pastor cannot give up the ministry. He fills in for others. But as he frequently has to change parishes, he is sorry that he can no longer keep a steady contact with those he meets. Retiring seems to him to be the antithesis of the Gospel. He questions the bureaucratic procedure by which, in Christian circles, a man's destiny depends upon the laws of efficiency. In reality, it is toward the end of life that the insights gained by long experience are harvested. If the ministry is interrupted, the mainspring runs down. A man remains alert and energetic when he knows his life will continue to be of value to God and to others until his dying breath.

22 April
The little lamb is dead. The peasant in me is deeply affected.

23 April
Mealtime conversation with Oscar. This boy from Burundi has just learned of his father's death. He does not know the circumstances. This morning he came running up to talk about it, his face lined with grief. After the Eucharist celebrated in memory of his father, we attempted to exchange a few words. What could we say? Oscar is the head of the family, and his exile prevents him from joining his relatives. Listening to him brings to life the nightmare a large part of Africa is going through. He is cut off from his country, for how long he has no idea. To console him by speaking of the day when he will see his family once more would be to plunge him into illusion. Are we going to be passive spectators of the tragedy of so many nations? At the very thought, a gaping void opens before us.

26 April
A mild night, In the distance, through the white mist lit by the full moon, the outlines of the hills of Cortambert and Bray are visible. Happiness: there it is, within reach. Never seek it, it would only flee. It lies in attentiveness and in wonder. Happiness seems sometimes to disappear for a long, long time. And yet there it is, when eyes meet. There it is, close at hand, when a man loves, without really knowing if he is loved in return. And if, as well, this man can feel that many love him, then he ought to be filled with a happiness beyond words. . . .

29 April
The parents of Alois tell how after the war, they had to leave the village in Eastern Europe where their families had lived for two centuries. The parents of both of them did not survive being up-rooted from country life. And their own roots, too, are still in the village where they were born. What kept them going? The father replies without a moment's hesitation: prayer. And Alois adds: it was a repetitive prayer, the rosary.

30 April
End of a thirty years' war in Indochina. How can I not hear once again the voice of the Vietnamese man from Hue who was here shortly before he died in the bombings, and who prayed in our church: "Lord, I am afraid of my fear."

5 May
Letter to a great-niece: "You know, you are dearly loved by your family, your uncle Roger included. You are loved, you and each member of your family, by God, and by Jesus Christ, for always. Now that you receive him in the Eucharist, you can be sure that he is offering you a fountain of living water. You will understand this little by little. But, as for the Eucharist, you will always receive it with the heart of a child, whatever your age."

10 May
Enchanting, all that the eyes take in. The coolness of the brief showers. Sunshine again, and each blade of grass has come alive. The happiness of the springtimes of childhood. Setbacks and shadows are washed by the fine rain, swept away by the hot light of a copper sunbeam. And the race begins all over again, leaps for joy alternating with expectations disappointed. In these little things a zest for life is engraved like filigree, a source without which everything would be insipid.

12 May
For my sixtieth birthday, my sister Genevieve prepared a meal with

all her household. The food was simple, but we stayed at table for a long time. Is it still possible to laugh so much, at our age? Aunt Mathilde, at ninety-four, too deaf to hear everything, laughed to see us laughing.

14 May

Gregoire and Johan set off to spend four months in Finland. Even in the far north of the country, young people are waiting for them. This arouses a little apprehension. So we tell each other: instead of being too concerned, supposing we look on the coming months as poems of communion?

18 May

Christian Precht has arrived, the Chilean priest who organizes all the efforts for mutual aid among the poor after the coup d'état. In the midst of serious tensions he has to solve thorny problems.

Together we discussed in what ways we could be in solidarity. At this very moment winter is setting in in Chile, with rain, dampness and cold. We cannot remain indifferent to a kind of genocide of women and children which comes with the winter months.

25 May

On Piekary Hill, near Cracow, pilgrimage of a hundred and eighty thousand men who work in the mines of Upper Silesia. They arrived this morning, long processions of them. First they received Communion during the night in their various parishes, then they set out in coaches and trains, finishing their journey on foot. The women will be waiting for them in the parishes when they return this evening. Invited to speak to them on prayer just after Cardinal Wojtyla's sermon, among other things I entrusted this intention to them: so many priests in Western Europe are isolated, while in Poland priests are supported by a whole nation of believers.

The Polish people has a unique vocation. In the course of a thousand years of history, it has amassed a treasury of generosity and perseverance. The constancy of its faith sustains the hope of many Christians all over the world.

28 May
Letter to Aniela Urbanowicz:
"I am reliving the time spent in your home in Warsaw. In my mind's eye I can see the many tokens of your hospitality, the wild flowers and garden flowers in the shallow bowl on your table. I wish you could have seen the vast forest, so close to Russia, where we went at the end of our stay to take home an old peasant who had come by train to Warsaw for the sole purpose of meeting us. Would it be possible for the young man who drove us there to take you to see those landscapes and those skies, some of the most remarkable in Europe? I am going to sit down and write about those landscapes, and I think many will go to Poland to see them, and to listen to the silence of those woods where the singing of the birds takes on a surprising resonance."

This aged woman, who lost her husband and her daughter in the concentration camps, brings out the true selves of many people, young and not so young. Her trust awakens intuitions in them. Her welcome in Warsaw was quite exceptional.

2 June
Walk with Marc on the path by the oak of Mamre. A slight breeze from the east has been blowing since daybreak: like the wind in a ship's sail, it lends a lightness to everything, even to speech. Marc is talking about a boy from an Eastern European country. We have no news of him and his luminous face comes to memory, as if wafted by the breeze. And once again, the eternal question: "Why him?"

10 June
In a dream I sail along the coast of Chile, with its pitiful hovels made of mere branches. Since coming back from Latin America, its people are with me even deep in the night. If the resistance of the Polish people is exemplary, it is because they struggled against invaders for centuries, selection was made, characters were fashioned. But what is to become of the Chilean people, who have never in their history been forged in the fires of such trials?

12 June

Received these surprising lines from Pedro:

"Today an old Portuguese woman reported to me what she had heard in the course of an ecumenical meeting, from the lips of the president of a Protestant Church: 'At Taizé there are crucified men who have seen the truth but do not proclaim it, so as not to break the unity of the Church.'

I just had to send you these words."

12 July

Why are we hear on the hill, we brothers and the young who come week after week?

We are here to be taken hold of by God, worked upon by him and inwardly changed. This transformation cannot be effected overnight. Continually we have to be modified anew. It is by no means monotonous, this search for God!

Transformation for what purpose? To become capable of accepting wholeheartedly events easy to deal with as well as hard times and oppositions, always ready to go toward what lies ahead.

If we do not allow ourselves to be taken hold of, we should not be surprised that we understand nothing about God and consider him a mere object of curiosity or interminable discussions; our life turns round and round in a never-ending monologue with ourselves. We may be able to understand many aspects of life and of the world by ourselves, but it is not so with knowledge of God. We know him only when we allow ourselves to be taken hold of and worked on by him from within.

25 July

Letter to one of our brothers who is living among the poorest of the poor and whose courage is boundless: "My dearly loved brother, I keep reading and rereading your last letter. Your lines transmit, with uncommon force, a breath of life. Our little community, loved by God and even indulged by him in so many regards, is able, through some of its brothers, to go to the extremes of loving and to suffer with the outcasts of society. All your powers are called for and laid bare in the service of the poorest, to such an extend that even your health is affected."

4 August

Went to Mâcon with Patrick. Heavy traffic made us take the old road, the one we used to take in the early years, on our bicycles or on horseback. Everything invites us to go frolicking, the little valleys running around the vineyards of the Mâconnais, the forests stretching as far as the valley of the Saône, the narrow road, squeezed in between hedges, woods, then fields and houses with their long galleries. But, spurred on by work, we are torn from our unfinished dreams and the car seems to sprout wings and fly. On our return, Taizé comes into view clinging to its hill, supported on its rocky foundations, against a dazzling sky, incandescent with the sun's heat. The constant need to admire is satisfied.

6 August

Today, as we celebrate the Transfiguration of Christ, we sing at the same time the unimaginable prospect of our own transfiguration. Christ enters us, and changes us into his likeness. He transfigures everything in us, the good as well as the bad.

In every man and woman there is a wound, inflicted by failures, humiliations, and the guilty conscience aggravated by moral injunctions and psychological explanations of every sort. This wound may have been caused at a time when we needed infinite understanding, and nobody was there to give it.

Moan about this wound and it becomes a torment, an aggressive force against ourselves and against others, generally against those who are closest to us.

Transfigured by Christ, it is changed into a locus of energy, a source of creativity giving rise to a potential for communion, friendship, and understanding.

7 August

Thought again intensely about those women we met in Poland, peasants who told of their six years of deportation along with their children in the camps of Siberia. To one of them, a humble peasant woman, I said, "You lived the martyrdom of Jesus Christ." In simplicity of heart she answered with one word: "Yes." That visit to a Polish village is one of the events a man experiences only once in his life. If there is any harmony still to be found on this earth, we owe it to those who have made the hidden offering of their lives, for the Church and for humanity.

14 August

> Murder of my soul,
> swallowed in dark desert nights.
> My being, silence;
> come back, Jesus.

Letting the pen run on produces these strange accents. Latent puritanism constantly desires to kill life; it is ashamed of spontaneity; it wants to murder the soul, disguising as positive injunctions what is only destructive violence.

17 August

Many older people have been invited by the young to spend a day at Taizé. It is so true that Christian communion is like an invitation to a meal prepared for all, without exception.

Now everywhere in the world, we are discovering people who have been forgotten, who are missing from the feast. Some can be found in old Churches, women and men who are waiting for Christ but who remain alone. Among them are many shepherds of the flock, priests or pastors who suffer intensely from isolation, who are so abandoned that they even wonder what good their ministry is.

This festival of communion would not be complete if we did not find some way of including those who, though nonbelievers, are our brothers and sisters. It is up to us to welcome them without ever making any of them feel that they are being trapped.

19 September

Tirelessly Christ seeks us and is at work in us. He keeps on asking: Do you love me? Do you love me more than anyone else?

That is because our relationship with him is one of friendship. And just as all friendship knows periods of indifference, in our life there are times of indifference to Christ. And then we wonder: have we left him?

No friendship can grow without new beginnings, reconciliations. When we are reconciled with Christ, we discover him as if for the first time: the love of all loves, maltreated, wounded, rejected by many and yet never tired of accompanying us.

Our Companion on the Way

On the evening of his resurrection, Jesus accompanied two of his disciples, on their way to the village of Emmaus. But at the time they did not realize it was Jesus.

There are times in our lives too, when we are unable to grasp that he is walking along with us. Yet whether we recognize him or not, whether we sense his presence or refuse it, he is there, even when we have no possible reason for hoping so. In the silence of our hearts he prays within us, in implicit prayer.

At other times, we are aware that he is with us and we want to talk to him. Then our prayer is explicit. "Show us the way," we ask; and he answers, "I am here." Again we say, "Listen, listen to my prayer, the prayer of a child." And our praying remains simple throughout our lives, like the prayers of childhood.

Why should we force our lips to formulate prayers at times when our whole being objects? If mind and heart can temporarily express nothing, the prayer of the body takes over, to indicate an intention, or else to surrender to God's silence. Luke's Gospel comes to an end with the image of the disciples bowed low to the ground, praying with their foreheads touching the earth.

There is a whole language for communicating with God. It consists of gestures, of intentions, of everything that emanates from ourselves. This in itself may not yet be prayer, but it is the self already on its way to being unified. Sowing the wheat in our field, leaving for work in the morning, caring for the sick, listening to others, writing, studying to become qualified—all this can become communication with God.

And the days will come once more when our passion for God is expressed in an overflowing heart, boundless imagination, and a song sung over and over again.

In this way times of ardent searching for God and times of intense everyday activity gradually become one. Prayer and life merge to form a single reality.

Prayer, whether implicit or explicit, brings peace and repose to the depths of our being.

Knowing where to find rest for our hearts means no longer lamenting over our unworthiness, over the possible tyranny of the self. It means no longer lingering over the contradictions of our personalities, in incessant self-analysis.

Knowing where to find rest for our hearts means grasping a reality hidden from our eyes: Christ is our companion on the way. And as a result, our burdened hearts begin to live again. They begin to sing, sometimes even without a sound: the breath of your love has visited me; I am no longer rooted to the spot; I am walking along with you.

PRAYER

Like your disciples
on the road to Emmaus,
we are so often incapable
of seeing that you, O Christ,
are our companion on the way.
But when our eyes are opened
we realize that you were speaking to us
even though perhaps we had forgotten you.
Then the sign of our trust in you
is that, in our turn, we try to love,
to forgive with you.
Independent of our doubts
or even of our faith,
O Christ, you are always there:
your love burns in our heart of hearts.

Journal: 20 September 1975–29 January 1976

20 September
One day Saint Teresa of Avila and Saint John of the Cross met for
a meal. Grapes were brought in. "I'm not going to eat any," said
John of the Cross. "Too many people have none." Teresa answered, "I, on the contrary, am going to eat them, to praise God
for these grapes." Their conversation mirrors one of the tensions
of the contemporary Church.

21 September
Discover fragments of humanity in the most dehumanized, flashes
of generosity in the most hostile.

22 September
Talked with a couple. They are in major difficulty with two of
their children. What can be done to help them through their troubles? How to convince them that if their children have grown apart
from them and even from God, they need not worry about their
future? They have already given them the best of themselves by a
kind of osmosis, and this best will come out when the children take
on responsibilities in life, perhaps when they in turn educate their
own children. Then they will have to sift all they have assimilated
and it is the very best, the pure wheat handed down from their
parents, that they will retain.

23 September
Be attentive to the silences of God. They are often more tangible
than his signs.

24 September
Long conversations with Martin. His mission among the poorest is
going to take him far. He will be so alone, in the center of Africa.
In spite of the value of a departure like this, the heart's reasons
count for more and make every long absence of a brother hard to

bear. Only the confidence of faith allows us to consent to such missions.

11 October
It can happen that someone discovers violence against father or mother in his heart. Generally speaking, these feelings are not exteriorized in words, and this is just as well. All human beings are inhabited by urges which can be quite drastic. If people expressed all their latent aggressiveness to one another, it would be disastrous. Violence and jealously are in the human heart. Stirring up these murky waters in the name of sincerity and truth leads only to loss of vitality and energy. That should be kept for our dialogue with a man who has received the ministry of declaring God's forgiveness.

12 October
Communion in the Church is sometimes threatened by those who wield ecclesial authority in order to assert themselves, in extreme cases, to compensate for some frustration.

But there are also shepherds who have persevered in a whole lifetime of faithfulness. Sometimes their ministry has only been exercised for a small number, recognized only by a few. Aware of the feeble resonance of their priesthood, they arouse our admiration. What words can be found to tell them to what degree they are the salt of the earth? Often these words stick in our throat, and perhaps better so: the value of the gift of their lives is indescribable.

23 October
What do you wish for your brothers? Freedom. Not an autonomy that would make individualists of them, but the freedom of communion, the freedom that does not infringe upon the liberty of another.

24 October
A flowering of contemplative vocations would raise the hopes of a Church in mourning.

9 November
Two children, in dark clothes, arrive timidly at the church. Six and eight years old. Their names, Marie and Henri. We open a picture-book at the page where there are two children and I tell them: here are Marie and Henri, and close beside them, Jesus. Then we discuss who to pray for. The next day, Marie talks to her parents and insists that the family stay till the evening prayer. As that is impossible, she comes out with: "It wasn't worth it, being here for only one day; better not to have come at all." After that, how can we fail to let the prayer of children show us grown-ups the way, we who are so ready to believe that prayer must pass through the intelligence, be explicit and logical?

14 November
Came across this Chinese proverb: "If you want to work for a year, sow wheat; for ten years, plant a tree; for thirty years, train men."

15 November
Maria de Lourdes Pintasilgo, Portugal's representative at UNESCO is spending a few days at Taizé. We are still hoping for a springtime of Lisbon. Such a springtime is essential if the younger generations in Europe are to keep alive their hope in humanity. They are tired of so many political experiments that, one after another, have come to nothing.

16 November
The Chilean government has just dissolved the "Committee for Peace." Immediately sent this message to Cardinal Silva, the archbishop of Santiago:
"After my journey to Chile, I kept quiet. Today, after the dissolution of the Committee for Peace by the Chilean government, I cannot keep silent. In Santiago I saw with my own eyes the work done with unflagging courage by this committee, to give aid to the most destitute and hope to those in despair, especially children. I

have confidence in your powers of discernment to find ways of continuing this work. With so many others in Chile you are a living witness to the Risen Christ, in agony until the end of the world. Be assured of my faithful support."

20 November
In the period before I was twenty, I was plagued by the fear of lacking in intellectual honesty. I refused to affirm a faith I could only dimly sense. But I was searching. And one day I came upon this verse of a Psalm: "My heart says of you: seek his face. I am seeking your face, O God." All of a sudden I realized that I could kneel down by my bed and say that very prayer: everything within me says, seek his face; I am seeking your face.

28 November
A few moments spent with Denis. His room has lost the look of an architect's office; the weaving loom has replaced the machine for copying blueprints. This brother, who took first place in the College of Architecture's final examinations, is unemployed. The office where he worked has no orders now. Intelligence is engraved on his features. He is still young, but like so many others these days, he has been forced for the time being to stop using skills that took so long to acquire.

6 December
Impossible to leave for Rome this year without thinking of the words our brother Christophe spoke eighteen months ago in an ecumenical meeting in Geneva, a few hours before the stroke which was to cause his death: "The year 1975 will be both the year of the General Assembly of the World Council of Churches and the Holy Year, which Pope Paul VI would like to make a year of reconciliation. May reconciliation remain at the heart of our searching." Those were the last words of that contemplative.

17 December

Finished the letter to the Pope, which I will put into the hands of Paul VI tomorrow:

"In order to move out of one of the impasses of ecumenism, for years now we have seen the necessity of living in a communion of love and trust, in spite of centuries of separation, with the Pope, the Bishop of Rome.

"Concerning the ministry of the Bishop of Rome, I have been led, in the course of these years, to sum up as follows the hopes and expectations of many:

"Firstly, people want the universal pastor to be concerned about justice among men and in the Church. It is up to him, therefore, to show not only the Catholic Church, but the non-Catholic Churches as well, the way towards great simplicity of means and the refusal to rely, in their march forward, on economic or political powers.

"Secondly, people also want the Bishop of Rome to do all he can to enable the reconciliations of Christians to come about without asking non-Catholics to deny their families of origin. Even with a view to a communion that is more universal, more ecumenical, truly catholic, denying is contrary to love. Even in the interests of a greater love, people cannot, in conscience, wound their love for those who brought them to birth in the faith. Among those who handed down the faith to them, there is very often a father and a mother. Could the Bishop of Rome, then, open the Eucharist to any baptized Christian who believes in the real presence of the Body and Blood of Christ, and who passionately seeks the unanimity of the faith, without requiring any denial from him? (Today I would write: . . . without asking him to be a symbol of denial.)

"Now at the end of this year of reconciliation, I have come to Rome with one specific intention. In the search for reconciliation among Christians and among all people, it is imperative to find simple but tangible gestures to accompany words of reconciliation.

"For years now you, as universal pastor, have asked forgiveness, if any blame could be attributed to you for the separation of baptized Christians.

"For this reason we from Taizé, together with many other people, earnestly desire one thing: to ask forgiveness of the universal pastor, the Bishop of Rome, for ancient or recent divisions among Christians, as well as for the delays in the search for reconciliation.

"Ours is a poor voice with little authority. It is by no means adequate to reply to your words. And yet, to keep silent in this year of reconciliation seems to me a betrayal of the Gospel.

"Is it not essential to devote all our energies to continuing the Holy Year by concrete gestures of ecumenical reconciliation, gestures that the Holy Spirit will indicate in response to our ardent searching?"

18 December
Audience with Paul VI. As I usually do in these intense conversations with the Pope, I brace myself against his writing table. Like any good countryman, once the body is firmly in place, the dialogue can get going. Following the method Paul VI likes, I have prepared a report, which he has already read, and on which we will base our conversation.

At the end of every audience, the Pope indicates that the meeting is over by taking in his hands the gift he has prepared. This year it is a photocopy of a ninth-century missal. Then the Pope, a man not spontaneous by nature, concludes for the first time by saying: "I am going to embrace you."

24 December
Invited to stay on in Rome for the Christmas Midnight Mass, celebrated by the Pope to mark the end of the Holy Year. This unexpected extension affords the chance to welcome some people from Lebanon. We search together with them: since words can do nothing to extinguish the waves of passionate hatred that are breaking over their country, could there be another way? And how to love those minorities who feel threatened? How to love those ma-

jorities who imagine that the solution lies in their superior force? How to understand the man who has lost all sense of direction and who explodes into the violence of words, or even of weapons?

3 January
Commit everything to him, with the heart of a child. Abandon yourself to him. Entrust to him all that goes against your heart or upsets your plans; pray for your opponent. And sometimes even go so far as to cry out your pain, when trials abound. Dare to use blunt, strong language: he understands it, even if others cannot. Entrust to him now and always whatever disturbs and torments you. And, keep silence in his presence.

Then, little by little, the praise of his love becomes the only thing that matters. Play within me, organs and zithers. Flutes, sing in me. Soft sounds and jubilant music, all together: let nothing stop the indispensable praise of his love.

9 January
It is rare to find people who do not worry about the poor quality of their praying. In vain Christ assures us that we do not add one second to our lives by worrying—we torment ourselves for not knowing how to pray.

10 January
For two days now, my sister M.-L. has been hovering between life and death. The victim of a car accident on her way to Taizé, her body is broken everywhere; she has eleven fractures. The breath of God unites in one and the same rhythm her breathing as she suffers in her hospital room, and mine as I go about my daily tasks.

20 January
Muslims and Christians, brothers of ours, are killing one another in Lebanon. A month ago a twenty-two-year-old Lebanese man, going back to his village to spend Chritmas there, was killed on the road in an ambush. The young martyr had a presentiment that he

was going to die. In his room at college he had left a letter to his family:

"I have just one request: forgive with all your hearts those who killed me. Join me in praying that my blood, even though I am a sinner, may help to atone for the sin of Lebanon. Mingled with the blood of all who have fallen, from all sides and from all the religious confessions, may it be offered as the price of the peace, the love and the concord which have disappeared from this country, and even from the whole world. Don't be afraid. What grieves me is that you will be sad. Pray, pray and love your enemies."

29 January

Annual council meeting of the community. We remind ourselves that we walk along a narrow ridge. Our vocation sets us on a knife-edge path. Day after day we face alternatives that bear the names: mediocrity or holiness, stagnation or the freshness of the Gospel, personal security or leaving all for Christ's sake.

We make our way along a ridge, at the risk of feeling the attraction of the void and losing our balance. Keeping on through thick and thin, without slipping down on one side or the other. Although it may mean bruises, sometimes even being torn apart, our vocation is to stand at the intersection of currents and conflicts, in that unique communion called the Church.

That Unique Communion
Called the Church

Weaving the Robe of Christ

Over the past fifteen years, new separations between Christians have been added to the old divisions of history. Many have lost interest in a visible communion of the People of God, to such an extent that the glorification of splits and oppositions has at times even become a new orthodoxy.

How aware are we that when divisions have occurred, there comes a time when it is too late to stop the process of splitting up? Freeing ourselves from suspicion in order to reconcile human beings who are torn apart involves a struggle to begin over and over again in transparency of heart, far from all dealing, scheming, and self-interested calculations.

Searching for reconciliation, of course, never means taking the easy way out. If it put people to sleep, anesthetized their energies, led them to a suffocating resignation, it would be the very opposite of reconciliation.

The ecumenical vocation had the mission of brnging together separated Christians, But after some real advances, things came to a standstill. Ecumenical dialogues went on and on, setting Christians on parallel tracks, and nothing more.

Today, the current which glorified oppositions is losing force, and so the ecumenical vocation could find a way out of its impasse. But we are still in the desert.... In the aridity of the desert, God speaks, but the language he speaks is his language, not ours.

Some people, often sincerely concerned with finding a way out of the impasse, resolutely entered upon ways that cut them off from the rest of the People of God.

For the same reason, others sent up trial balloons. They were aware of the risks involved—these balloons might explode as they gained height. But their principal concern was to remain at the heart of God's People, in order to bring it new life from within.

The attempt to make communion among Christians visible involves remaining on the inside, just as a human being can only be changed from within, never by criticisms coming from without. Harshness and pressures have always been stepping stones to blackmail, an attack on human freedom.

Recreating bonds of communion means weaving threads, sometimes just a single thread, but that is already enough. Then what is being woven, whether we know it or not, is the robe of Christ, his Church.

A Communion Extended to All Dimensions

Why are we so concerned about that unique communion called the Church? It is because there can be no continuity of Christ in human history without Christians who are part of a people. Loving Christ in isolation closes us up in our own private world. Loving Christ, loving the communion in his Body, the Church, opens unlimited vistas before us.

And why are we so passionately concerned about the catholicity of the Church, that universality extended to all its dimensions: the dimension of depth, which is the search for a face-to-face encounter in contemplation; the dimension of breadth, which is solidarity with man victim of man; the dimension of height, which is creativity in simple beauty, in common prayer?

This catholicity does not concern us on its own account. As soon as the Church becomes an end in itself, it is doomed to pettiness, to all kinds of definitive judgments that split it up into fragments—into confessions, small or large.

The Church does not interest us on her own account, but only when she stimulates us to look for God at the wellsprings of adoration, when she motivates us to live Christ for others and when she becomes a place of communion for all humanity.

That unique communion called the Church holds no interest for us unless it is universal, ecumenical, catholic, able to take upon itself the distress and the hope of the whole human community. Not a place reserved for a few privileged people, for elites of the faith, but one which is open to all of us, the poor of this earth.

No matter how open it is, of course, the church has contours, the contours of a body. But it holds no interest unless those who make it up are brothers and sisters of all, including nonbelievers.

Sources of Unanimity of the Faith

Today the Church is faced with one of the great challenges of her history: Is she sufficiently aware that she remains the only place capable of being a ferment of universal communion and of friendship in the human family as a whole?

For this ferment to reach all humanity, there is a prerequisite: a reconciliation between Christians that comes about without delay. How can unreconciled people profess allegiance to a God of love and awaken others to God by the lives they lead? Can Christians honestly continue to talk about ecumenism if they do not achieve reconciliation, concretely and without delay? If they only love those who love them and who resemble them, are not unbelievers capable of doing as much? The inconsistency represented by the divisions between Christians makes their words hardly credible, and turns the younger generations away from the Church.

When two separated individuals try to come together, it is essential for each of them first of all to discover the specific gifts placed in their partner. If each one claims to possess all the gifts and wants to bring everything and receive nothing, there will never be any reconciliation.

The same thing is true for separated Christians. Reconciliation does not mean that some are victorious while others are humiliated. It does not imply denying those who have transmitted faith in Christ to us; it too involves discovering the gifts placed in the others.

Will the communities born of the Reformation, then, become attentive to that source of unanimity in the Catholic Church, which is the Eucharist? Through thick and thin, the Catholic Church has allowed the Eucharist to remain a focus of unanimity of the faith, like an underground river flowing through her entire history, even the darkest periods (whereas it has always been in the nature of Protestantism to allow each individual the possibility of a personal interpretation of the words of Christ, including those concerning the Eucharist).

Adorable presence of Christ in the bread and wine, the Eucharist cannot be received mechanically, out of habit, but always in a spirit of poverty and repentance of heart, with the soul of a child, until the very evening of our years. When Pope Pius X, at the beginning of this century, opened the Eucharist even to children, he showed rare intuition.

The Eucharist is there for those who are starving for Christ. When a baptized Christian is hungry for the Eucharist and wishes to approach it, when Christ calls him, who would dare turn him away?

In remaining before the Eucharist during long inner silences when nothing seems to be happening, many people have matured the great decisions of an entire lifetime. They let themselves be penetrated down to the very depths of their beings, down to what we call the unconscious.

"My Kingdom is within you": even when the heart senses nothing, the Eucharist constantly brings to life these words of Christ, even for someone who hardly dares imagine it.

The Catholic Church is above all the Church of the Eucharist, but she has another special gift. She has known how to set apart men to bestow forgiveness, to loose on earth what is immediately loosed in the Kingdom, to lift from our shoulders the burden too heavy to bear, to wipe away the past, even the most recent past.

Confession gives us the opportunity of expressing as spontaneously as possible all that weights on our conscience. No one is able to say all there is to say about his faults. But if we say what springs to mind at the moment, that in itself is tremendous; it enables us to receive in the sacrament of reconciliation the unimaginable forgiveness of God.

In our time some people have felt that, to eliminate guilt feelings, it was necessary to play down or even to deny the reality of sin. But it has become clear that such an attitude, far from removing guilt, diffuses it through the whole being, spreads it out to such an extent that it cannot be reached, let alone uprooted.

Some, with great seriousness, make frequent use of confession, since they find it so necessary to live from this visible sign that wipes away all their past. Others, just as serious, make less frequent use of it, since they are so sure that God holds them in his forgiveness.

In both cases confession, however clumsy it may be, is essential for rediscovering the freshness of the Gospel, for entering a new birth. It teaches us to blow away our feelings of remorse even, like a child blowing away a dead leaf. This is God's happiness, the dawning of perfect joy.

As for the Protestant Churches, their specific gift has been to be above all the Churches of the Word. The Catholic Church too has always found in Scripture a source for living a life centered on God. But will Catholics recognize that the best of Protestantism was to have discovered the impact of the Word of God in personal life?

This word from God must be situated in Scripture as a whole, not taken in isolation; it is essential to put it into practice immediately.

If we remember the quality of some of the great Protestant divines of the seventeenth and eighteenth centuries, those whose writings and poems were turned by Johann Sebastian Bach, for example, into chorales and hymns of an intensity rarely achieved, then we can better understand to what extent the Word of God was loved and taken seriously in personal living, how it stimulated a whole inner life, how it met, stirred, and worked through the Protestant Christian down to his very depths.

A Church Devoid of Powerful Means

Some members of the younger generation love the Church, but with a blind passion. And so they are deeply disturbed when they see individual Christians, or institutions, quick to profit from the ease offered by abundant material resources, be they buildings, capital held in reserve, or financial investments.

Long before Christ's coming, the prophet Jeremiah pronounced these challenging words: "My people have abandoned the source of living water; they have exchanged the radiance of God for cisterns that cannot hold water." And today there are young people who ask themselves similar questions. Is the absolute of God, his radiance, being exchanged for cisterns that do not contain living water? Whether in the short or in the long run, powerful means and authoritarian methods mean the death of communion.

The young are no more simplistic than their elders. It is not a matter of rejecting the display of artistic splendor in churches built down through the ages. When there is no artistic creation, puritanical and sectarian tendencies develop; they dehumanize and put pressure on people by creating guilty consciences. It is, rather, a matter of disposing everything in creation's simple beauty, and art too is a gift from God. Simplicity of means need not lead to drab expressions where the dull, the conventional, and the monotonous exude boredom.

And using simple means, of course, does not entail rejecting certain indispensable means for communicating across the world.

But for the younger generation, what is going to matter is for the Church to lead them to a source from which wonder and astonishment are continually springing up afresh. For the young the Church is recognizable when it is a place where Christians are not trying to

survive at all costs, but to be born and reborn. The Church is
recognizable when it touches the whole of their being, body and
spirit. Then it captivates, then it leads us to take risks, and still
more risks, for Christ's sake and the Gospel's, until our dying day.

PRAYER

Lord Christ,
the mystery of your presence is beyond price,
and mysterious the road on which you wait
to lead us to the Father.
Even when we understand
so little of your life,
your Spirit who dwells in our hearts
makes God
comprehensible to us.
And so you work a miracle:
you make us into living stones
in your body, your Church.
O Christ, you are Love,
and you do not want us to be judges
who stand on the outside and condemn,
but rather leaven in the dough
of every community,
and of the human family—
a ferment able to raise the enormous weight
of all that has become stiff and hardened.

Journal: 24 February–11 November 1976

24 February

> Heart of my shattered heart,
> who will soothe the buried lament?
> Who will pour oil on the biting pang
> that never dies?
> Christ, do you hear the words held back?
> You are there, a love most soothing.

When all within is serene, why these lines? Certain that the years to come will be for singing God.

21 March
Writing so many letters means living so intensely with each correspondent that it would scarcely be a surprise, on raising my head, to meet his gaze above the page. The pen runs on, swiftly, and the heart causes it to discover as it runs what the mind had no inkling of a moment before. No point in rereading letters, if words or ideas miss the mark never mind, rereading would take away the spontaneity of the first flow and steal precious time from the writing of more letters.

25 March
A young Protestant asks me how to face the dryness, sometimes the emptiness, of his prayer. When, in his heart of hearts, a man knows that he is loved for ever and ever, he is not afraid to wait in silence, even if some silences were to last until death.

1 April
After attending the adoration of the Blessed Sacrament at Notre Dame in Paris, Leonard remarked: on such occasions you rediscover the great Catholic tradition of France, and you go away the greater for it.

4 April

A few days ago Fabienne came in with a sweater that her aunt, my sister Genevieve, had just washed. I offer her some dates and ask her what is happening at school, if she likes playing the harpsichord (she is very gifted), and, now that she is ten, if being the eldest of five brothers and sisters is not too much responsibility for her. To all these questions she replies only by nodding slightly and muttering, "Hmm, hmm." Why is she so shy? Was she scared by a dog on her way here? Her big laughing eyes give no clue. Next day her parents tell me she didn't know what to do with the date stones, so she kept them all in her mouth until she couldn't speak a word.

5 April

Meeting of young people in Brussels Cathedral. In these last few days, all the good reasons for escaping the ordeal of leaving Taizé to speak in public kept piling up—it is so much better to listen to individuals in personal conversations, it is so difficult to leave the many young people already here twelve days before Easter. It was a good idea, though, to agree to take part in this congress of the World Federation of Catholic Youth Movements, because we do so want the Council of Youth, far from serving itself, to have the vocation of offering a service to the Church, to tendencies that already exist or that are coming into being, to movements, to young people, priests, nuns, and brothers.

9 April

Surprising conversation with some university students from Iran, who had come to spend a week at Taizé. They are Muslims, but they speak the same language as so many young Western Christians: they do not go to the mosques, for they consider practicing Muslims to be merely conformists. They will be looking for ways of arranging little corners for prayer in the mosques when they return home.

14 April

This morning the hill is resting under a great woolly sky, a vast fleecy rug with patches of vivid blue. In the wood the charred undergrowth has given place to a riot of gold against brilliant green: a kind of ranunculus with jagged petals has spread into the farthest corners. But this enchantment is short-lived.

15 April

Many discussions with young people in preparation for Easter. In the course of the winter, there has been enthusiastic searching after new ideas for the next stage on our way forward. Some were responsible for reading and listening to the many suggestions that came in from everywhere. Some days their heads were full to bursting!

We are aware of the tremendous tensions that are shaking our societies. In the midst of a situation where sclerosis is setting in, it is important to open up ways toward a hope rooted in Christ, the hope of believers, and toward a human hope, one we share with nonbelievers.

How can we fill up the chasms dug by big vested interests, the powers of this world, who assert themselves by restricting or suppressing human freedom, and to this end use every means, including political imprisonment and physical and moral torture?

To counteract the effects of injustice and hatred, those inexorable driving forces of history, we do not have the powerful weapons of war at our disposal, but only the violence of peacemakers, the violence of those on fire who take possession of the realities of the Kingdom of God.

To live out all that lies before us, we will continue using poor means, a minimum of organization, and no bureaucracy; we will continue to refuse donations. It is so ture that the moment you yield an inch in this regard, you wake up one fine morning compromised, at the mercy of financial interests.

17 April

Easter Eve. What sign can we announce to all the young people who have come from many different countries, to say that there is only one human community, and that the rifts growing deeper between North and South are breaking up this human family?

Next October, we will go with an intercontinental group of young people to share the life of the poorest of the poor, in Calcutta and then in Bangladesh. It is only a limited gesture, a poor parable, but it shows in which direction we are heading.

In order to find ways of being a ferment of communion in a human community that is under increasing tension, it seems that the time has come to compose another letter to the People of God. We will write it in Asia.

23 April

In sending me the following lines, Johan thinks that his experience may illuminate others as well as himself:

"A fortnight after my return from Finland, as I was going into church one day, I suddenly saw God standing at the top of the choir steps. His arms were outstretched in a gesture of welcome and he radiated boundless love, a boundless longing to welcome each one, the ordinary as well as the saint. If it has taken me such a long time to write this down, it is because I needed time to assimilate an experience both strong and fleeting, and to realize that perhaps it did not happen for my benefit alone."

16 May

Turin. Coming here to speak at a gathering of young people also means seeing Cardinal Pellegrino again. In the midst of conflicts, he stands firm with infinite courage, at the cost, among other things, of being rejected by the powerful of this world. The ministry of this man, a son of the poor, is essential for the people of Piedmont. He has the insights so often granted to the very old. When I think of him I see him as a direct descendent of the Church Fathers. From the days of his consecration as a bishop, at which I was present, I realized that in him the Church had a man of the sources of the faith.

31 May
Rudolf passes by the window. A pile of letters in his arms—the mail from Germany. Just one day's letters, and each one has to be answered. It is not for nothing that some brothers work late into the night, although in the morning the bells call all of us without exception to prayer.

4 June
A few moments in the pottery. On a blackboard where the young brothers who work there are in the habit of writing a quotation, there are these words: "Your love, O Christ, has wounded my soul; I go forward singing your praises." Are they the authors of such a profound thought? No, it was written in the seventh century by John Climacus in his old age. At the age of fifteen, he had entered the monastery of Sinai. He realized that a passion for Christ is expressed through a man's whole being, flesh and spirit.

6 June
Eve of Pentecost. Late this evening in the church, a luminous face, features of extreme pallor under hair in silvery bandeaux. At the age of seventy-five, a woman says words that sum up the intention of multitudes of mothers and grandmothers: "I have come here to pray for those who are losing the faith, for my grandchildren."

4 July
Reading a lot about the USSR and the United States. Two fascinating countries. Russia, with her people able to survive the most severe trials, rooted and bound to their land, in love with nature as few others. The Americans: after uninterrupted successes, feverishly pursued, now tormented by an anxiety they have never before experienced. On this day when Americans celebrate the anniversary of their independence, it would be enthralling to be there, to

understand more. Next on the list, books about contemporary India. Underlying this constantly renewed interest in economics,
sociology, and the social sciences is one recurring question: Where
is God, where is Christ, where is the Gospel in all these nations?

5 July
Corrected the proofs of *A Life We Never Dared Hope For.* Select-
ing pages of a journal for publication is not a very appealing task.
Some of the brothers chose the pages of the manuscript to be kept,
the ones that comment, in detail or in general, on our ongoing life,
shot through by a hope against all hope. Like *Festival*, this new
book affords glimpses of a struggle to keep despair from getting
the upper hand.

14 July
Three o'clock in the morning. Short walk in the meadow. Several
times the cock gives his call. The crow wakes us and clumsily flies
from his perch down toward the wood. The silence, broken for a
moment by his hoarse croaking, closes in again. In the east, red
light begins to play on the crests of the Tournus hills.

3 August
At this time of year when so many young people are at Taizé, all
my inner resources are challenged by the same question as thirty-
six years ago. At that time, when I was called to lead a group of
Christian students, the question was already the same: How to let
people catch a glimpse of Christ, the poor man of Nazareth, whose
reflection is present in the heart of every individual?

Now, in high summer, the main thing is to find words, week
after week, to keep on telling people who this poor man of Nazareth is—the man who walks our ways of darkness and lights them
up, whenever we let him look through our eyes. How often it might
be tempting to give up this weekly meeting with all the people on
the hill. How is it possible to talk about him every week with fresh
words? Will those who listen understand that he is alive, that he

lives within them? Will they realize that he is knocking at their door?

5 August

As I write, a tiny beetle manages to climb up on my motionless left hand; he crawls along my arm, his dark stiff back gleaming with rich colors.

My joy in creation is ever present. As the days go by, it becomes indistinguishable from that other joy, communion with people. But, without a Presence more certain than all earthly realities, none of this happiness would remain.

Amidst the pressures of work and of meetings, sometimes when tempers flare, when urgent matters continually interrupt the work in hand, he is there, the One who sets us free.

17 August

Yesterday, visit from Mother Teresa of Calcutta. Together we composed a prayer:

"O God, the Father of everybody, you ask us all to bring love where the poor are humiliated, joy where the Church is downcast, and reconciliation where people are divided—fathers and sons, mothers and daughters, husbands and wives, believers and those who cannot believe, Christians and their unwanted fellow Christians. You open this way for us, so that the broken body of Jesus Christ, your Church, may be leaven of communion for the poor of the earth and in the whole human family."

10 September

Fields and woods hold festival, the light dances between fleecy dawns and sunsets, softer with every day. The festival goes on, with no end in sight. Yesterday someone said there had been too much precipitation in the last month, and yet only two or three heavy showers come to mind. At the end of the meadow, under the almond tree, there is hardly enough shade to sit in this morning. Down below, the vineyard, growing vigorously in its third year, is already laden with purplish grapes, promising well for its first wine.

19 October

In the life of the Church the shepherd, the one who is at the heart of the living cell which a community is, has only one charge, to be the servant of communion. He is there to try to keep alive what otherwise would dislocate and scatter, to the point where one day the community would no longer be one.

On this eve of the departure for Calcutta, I reminded my brothers that, from the very beginning, I have never wanted to be called "prior" within the community. I am their brother. And in the last few years we have seen to it that outside the community, too, the name "prior" is only used in certain situations, to identify rapidly a particular charge.

For the same reason, years ago, I refused the Legion of Honor. Why? Because today it is impossible for those holding positions of responsibility in the Church to add honorific titles to their service of God. They can no longer permit honors to be attached to pastoral office.

24 October

In the plane, bound for India. The meetings these last two evenings in the Stiftskirche of Tubingen, that church which is so symbolic of German Protestantism, and in the splendid cathedral of Munster, fill the heart to overflowing. The churches full of young people, the journey through Germany so far beyond anything we could have imagined: only the angels could find words for it. The friendship and the mutual trust between us and so many young Germans is a real force.

Through my words, even poorer than on other occasions, did they understand that anyone, of whatever age, who is willing to take risks for Christ and for the Gospel, is led, sometimes in spite of himself, to share in the most unexpected adventures?

31 October
Fraternal welcome at Calcutta airport. In Indian fashion, young people had prepared the garlands of flowers that they always hang around the neck of a new arrival.

We had decided to come and live in a district of Calcutta so that the letter to the People of God would be written among those who are familiar with the most widespread condition on earth, poverty.

The young people who went ahead of us, arriving from America, Africa, Europe, and from other Asian countries, already have a foothold. But they have had difficulty in finding a place to stay: families live in such crowded conditions, and the large colleges are not suitable for us. It was only yesterday they were told: there is a Catholic family, living in a very poor Muslim district, who will understand what you want.

And so here we are in the middle of this noisy neighborhood, full of children. Tonight we met the Joseph family. Living in three tiny rooms, they offered at first to accept only my four brothers and myself. Then they agreed that all the boys could stay here, sleeping on the ground. Finally the mother said the girls could sleep upstairs with her. They have eight children. They are beaming. We realize right away that beginning tomorrow, the eldest son could join our intercontinental team. They have understood everything already.

1 November
Early in the morning everyone leaves for work. I myself go to the home for children found in the street. One little girl of four months, with a solemn face, attracts my attention. She has no name. She lost her mother at birth. Sister Fabienne, who directs the home, says that this little girl ought to be taken to Europe, urgently: she is very delicate, winter will be coming soon, and she will certainly be among the fifty per cent of the children who have not the strength to survive the bad season with its epidemics. And she adds: take her, save her, you can see that she is already attached to you, yours is the first man's voice she has heard.

2 November
Work at the home for the dying. An old man, about to die, cannot manage to swallow. He asks us to pray for him. A young man, lying farther along, calls out. He makes a gesture with both hands indicating God, Allah, a look of profound intensity on his face. He lays his cheeks on my hands several times. He has great difficulty breathing.

In the afternoon, our first meeting together to prepare the letter to the People of God. We listen to those who have already gathered ideas together from everywhere, whether in Taizé or in the course of journeys through all the continents.

3 November
A little walk in the alleys. Mohammed Yacine comes up to us and asks why we are here. He talks about the neighborhood: twenty-five per cent of the people are unemployed, and half of those who have work have no steady employment. He offers us tea. Mohammed Ismael, the schoolteacher, turns up. At first he speaks aggressively, affirming that all we are saying is in the Koran too; he tells us that Muslims never abandon one of their own in need. The conversation continues. At the end of our meeting, he apologizes for having been hard on us; he thought we had come with political intentions. He invites us to come to his school to have a meeting with the men.

4 November
Starting today, an old Christian woman from the neighborhood is joining in our life and our thinking. She understands everything.

5 November
The temperature continues to be above normal, and the humidity at maximum. We all stand it wonderfully well, sustained as we are by the enthusiasm of our search. The nights are short, the street noises intense. Transistors blare out Indian songs. All this noise goes on late into the night and starts again at five in the morning,

when people begin to wash outside in the street by dousing themselves with water. The sewer flows past our courtyard gate; we have to cross it every time we go out and it has just begun to get wider.

In two or three days, a simplification of our life-style has taken place. The people of the neighborhood are surprised that foreigners are willing to sleep on the ground.

6 November

Mother Teresa has sent us a little wooden tabernacle, which we will use for the reserved Sacrament.

Visit to Pilkana, one of the largest slums of the city, seventy thousand inhabitants in an area seven hundred meters square. Human beings plunged into an ocean of tribulations.

Pilkana is that child, suffocating with tuberculosis, a Muslim. His mother says: he does nothing but pray now. Pilkana is the unforgettable beauty of the face of a young Christian woman with advanced tuberculosis of the bones who keeps repeating: today is a beautiful day. Pilkana is that old woman, dying on her doorstep, covered with putrefying sores.

Is it a collective sin that creates the existence of these Golgothas in a city replete with wealth?

8 November

From now on the young people of the team are working in small groups, in order to tackle a new topic every day: housing, prayer, work, possessions, the human family.

10 November

Received in Calcutta a letter from Latin America. A young man, the father of a family, announces that he has been set free from his political prison. He, his wife, and his two children will now go to live for a while with our brothers in Brazil:

"It was your brothers and all who live lives of prayer that I remembered most during all my time in prison. In my solitude I was deeply conscious of God's presence. Now we are very happy to be given hospitality by your brothers; we feel at home with them. I lived for fifty days blindfolded, my hands tied, spending some days with nothing or almost nothing to eat, unable to communicate with anyone at all. They released me on condition that I leave my country, but they did not say for how long. Keep on praying for us, and for all the prisoners. Many of my companions used to say to me, 'I am not a believer, but pray for me.' I understand the contemplative life more and more. God knows what he is doing and it will all bear fruit.''

11 November

With Mother Teresa, visited the leper hospital. On the way she explains why, in the very first days of our visit and without asking my advice, she had her sisters make me a second white robe. She doesn't understand why I don't wear it all day long. It is no good explaining that in Europe, it is difficult to wear outside in the street a garment for prayer. She insists: you should never take it off, people today need this sign. To which I reply: "I could not make that kind of decision without consulting my brothers."

In the leper hospital, the welcome from the hundreds of patients was striking in its spontaneity. They are all contagious. Many asked for the laying on of hands.

The Leper's Song

One question rises incessantly from the human heart: if God existed, he would not permit wars, injustice, illness, and the oppression of even one human being. If God existed, he would prevent man from doing evil.

In the course of two visits to a leper hospital in Calcutta, I saw a leper raise his arms and what remained of his hands and begin to sing these words: "God has not inflicted a punishment on me; I praise him because my illness has turned into a visit from God."

On either side of him, to be sure, other lepers were moaning with pain and with despair. But this one had realized that suffering is not sent by God, it is not the result of a misdeed, God is not the author of evil, he is neither a manipulator nor a tormentor of the human conscience.

Listening to the leper's song, I seemed to be hearing Job, that believer of long ago, before Christ, on whom trials rained down. Job knew that his immense suffering was not punishment for a fault: the innocent, devoid of guile, can be a victim just as well as the tyrant, the despot with a heart of stone. And one day, Job was able to say like the leper of Calcutta: "In my trials God seeks me; I know now that my Redeemer is alive, and my heart is burning within me."

But why does God not prevent man from doing evil? It is because he has not made human beings robots. He created us in his own image, that is, free.

When we love a human being with all our hearts, our love desires to leave the loved one free to respond with a similar love, but free as well to refuse.

In the same way God, who loves us with a love beyond words, leaves us free to make a radical choice: free to love but also to

179

refuse love and to reject God; free to spread through the world a leaven of reconciliation or a ferment of injustice; free to love or to hate; free to shine with radiant communion in Christ, but also to tear ourselves away from it and even to destroy in other people their thirst for the living God. He leaves us free, even to rebel against him.

But although God leaves us free, he does not look on passively at our distress. He suffers along with us. He visits us, even in the wilderness of our hearts, through Christ who is in agony for each and every human being on this earth.

PRAYER

O God,
you suffer at the death of your friends,
but you do not leave us
to founder in grief
at the death of those dear to us.
The death of those we love
pains you, O God.
Christ is in agony for every human being,
and through him, you suffer
with all who suffer times of trial.
And, through the Risen Christ,
you come to lighten the unbearable load;
you open our eyes to the wonder of a love.
In him, you are constantly saying:
"Come, follow me,
for I am gentle and humble of heart;
in me you will find rest,
and as you rest in me
you will know healing."

Journal: 13 November–31 December 1976

13 November
Leave for Bangladesh to visit our brothers. While the group of young people remain in Calcutta, I take away with me the ideas already sketched out for the letter to the People of God to consult the young people of Bangladesh.

14 November
To have brothers in Bangladesh, sharing the existence of people in a subhuman situation, is like seeing the flesh of our flesh become part of the poorest of people. The landscape is vividly beautiful, but housing conditions are beyond words.

Some forty young people have come from several parts of the country to meet us. With them we have long conversations and we take away with us Ranjan's question: "What way can we find to form one great human family?"

This country has behind it thirty years of troubles, from the bombings at the end of the Second World War to the catastrophic floods, not to forget the tragedies of the War of Independence.

16 November
Long conversations with my brothers on the meaning of their presence here.

Why do small groups of brothers plunge into slums in Asia, Africa, and Latin America, to live there for years, when we know that these districts are more and more closed to Westerners? And why, with an intercontinental group of young people, did we plunge into a similar neighborhood in Calcutta?

Our presence is never in order to revive the process which involves coming from the Northern hemisphere and bringing our own imported solutions, no matter how valuable they may be. We know all too well how wary the inhabitants of the Southern hemisphere are of any relationship of dependency. If we go to these places, we do so in order to live a presence with no ulterior motives.

To the question "do we go with absolutely no intention of accomplishing anything?" we would answer "no." Though we do not seek short-term effectiveness by bringing money or solutions worked out in the West, we do want to support local young people who are taking initiatives inspired not by us but by their own culture and their own genius, arising from the very depths of their own peoples. Such young men and women exist. They have concrete suggestions to offer. Like young Europeans, they are sometimes discouraged in the face of impossibilities, and in danger of falling into a scepticism that will lead them either to passivity or to violence.

We go to live with them in slums above all to live a parable of communion, always with only a minimum of material resources. And this in the presence of the reserved Sacrament, which turns a run-down shack into a place inhabited by a Presence. Immersing ourselves in slums means living in the same way as the inhabitants, and waiting with them for an event from God for their peoples.

17 November
At nightfall, a sufi came in for a few moments. He wanted to speak a final word before we left Bangladesh: "All men have the same Master. Now, that is still a secret, as yet unrevealed. But later it will be discovered." And he went away again into the night.

20 November
Calcutta. A morning's work among children. Spent a long time with the premature babies. One of them, weighing almost nothing, his face lined with deep wrinkles, wanted to cry but had no voice. His mouth opened and he wept noiselessly. To be with these dying babies, holding them close, feeling their weakness as they suffer their agony, is like having one's heart torn out. Some cannot even feel the loving presence beside them and yet they suffer.

21 November
Inwardly preoccupied about the letter to the People of God. To be-

gin with, we were in a thick fog. After some time our eyes began to see. How could we remain blind when every morning we were doing the kind of work we had to do? Our hearts beat very strongly, but we remained dumb. Then our lips began to speak. And now it is the hand, still unable to write it down. The fog has not completely lifted yet. Late this evening the solution came to us. We are going to give up entirely the attempt to write a text containing too many abstract ideas, keeping only the concrete proposals.

There are many children around. They have a sense of rhythm; they sing and they dance.

22 November

At the home for the dying, the young man of the other evening seems to be better. He is like a skeleton, but perhaps he can be saved.

Here, what can we give except first and foremost human love? Going from one to another, stopping to spend a few moments with each one, telling them they are our brothers, our friends or, the youngest, our sons. With them, the language of gesture is what counts. This morning a blind man kept placing my hands over his eyes. In laying our hands on them and praying with them, we have to remember their origins—Hindu, Muslim, or Christian.

It is true that in Europe we have our homes for the dying too. The only difference is that they are not obvious. When at Taizé I listen to many young people individually, I come across this or that one, the son or daughter of divorced parents, who in addition may be suffering from a broken heart: they are like the living dead. In the home for the dying, as I pass from one to another, I find myself at times in the same situation as in Taizé, when in the evening some of the young people wait their turn to come and say a few words to unburden themselves of their despair.

And not only the young, but also middle-aged and elderly people who in their lives have loved much and now find themselves overcome by loneliness, their lives devoid of meaning.

In the present crisis of confidence in man, how many are crushed by the mistrust of others, at those times when they are forced to recognize that their sincerest intentions have been distorted.

In our well-organized Europe, we too have our homes of the dying, but they are invisible.

25 November
Mass celebrated by Cardinal Picachy, archbishop of Calcutta. It takes only a few Bengali lamps to transform our courtyard into a palace from the Arabian Nights. People are everywhere, even on the roofs.

28 November
Yesterday, owing to the censorship imposed in India by the state of emergency, we could not send by telex the text of the letter to the People of God, so that it could be translated before our return for the gathering of young people at Notre Dame in Paris. That gave us extra time. We profited from it to add a few paragraphs of introduction: we had not yet found the words to explain why the essence of this letter was the parable of sharing. Today it has been done.

31 December
Since we came back from Calcutta, the little Indian girl we brought with us has been living in my room. At five and a half months, Marie-Sonaly is so delicate. She can only go to sleep in my arms. Day and night, it is amazing how she reacts to my voice.

Perhaps she has only a few more weeks to live. If she were to sense my growing anxiety for her life.... Then I say to myself: if she dies, then you will talk it out, you will even argue, alone with God. But for the time being, entrust her to God. Resting on your heart, she will at least have experienced that trust God has placed in each one of us, and which is transmitted through another human being. Let anguish be transfigured into confidence.

The Wonder of a Love

Letter from Africa

I wrote the following letter in November and December 1978, while living in a slum in Africa. Between it and the rest of this book there is thus a gap of two years. Texts from my journal during this interval will be published in a forthcoming book.

Some of my brothers chose the texts that make up this present book from among all my papers, and from among the prayers I compose each day for the midday prayer at Taizé.

You are seeking fulfillment, so from Africa I am writing you this letter. It is the sequel to another letter, *A life we never dared hope for.*

He Never Forces Anyone's Hand

You keep on asking me, "How can I find fulfillment?"

If only I could lay my hand on your shoulder and go with you along the way.

Both of us together, turning toward Him who, recognized or not, is your quiet companion, someone who never imposes himself.

Will you let him plant a source of refreshment deep within you? Or will you be so filled with shame that you say, "I am not good enough to have you near me?"

What fascinates in God is his humility. He never punishes, never domineers nor wounds human dignity. Any authoritarian gesture on our part disfigures his face and repels.

As for Christ, "poor and humble of heart"—he never forces anyone's hand.

If he forced himself upon you, I would not be inviting you to follow him.

In the silence of the heart, tirelessly he whispers to each of us, "Don't be afraid; I am here."

Dying and Rising with Jesus

To joy he calls us, not to gloom.

No groaning at the bonds that bind you, or the tyranny of a self you want to preserve. No drawing back into yourself, intent on mere survival, but at every stage in life, a new birth.

His joy not for your private possession, or all happiness would flee.

I would like to help you make your life a poem of love with him. Not a facile poem, but through the very greyness of your days, his joyfulness, even hilarity. Without him, how could there be fulfilment?

Whatever your doubts or your faith, he has already placed ahead of you what fires your enthusiasm.

Nobody can answer for you. You and you alone must dare.

But how?

Go to the ends of the earth and plunge into the conditions of those society rejects; overturn the powers of injustice; restore human dignity: is that taking risks? Yes, but that's not all there is to life.

Or again: sharing all you own, could that be the risk of the Gospel?

As you try to follow Christ, the day will come when you are irresistibly drawn to that. Responding will mean drinking deep at the unfailing springs. Anyone refusing to quench his thirst there first would become, unconsciously, a doctrinaire of sharing.

But what is the greatest risk to which this Man of humble heart invites everyone? It is "dying and rising with Jesus."

Passing with him from death to life; at times accompanying him in his agony for all the human family and, each day anew, beginning to rise from the dead with him.

Joyful, not overwhelmed. Every moment, leaving everything with him, even your weary body. And using no exotic methods, for then you would have lost the sense of praying.

Will you be able to wait for him when your heart cries out in loneliness, and the ultimate question is torn from your soul, "But where is God?"

Wait for him, even when body and spirit are dry and parched. Wait, too, with many others for an event to occur in man's present day. An event which is neither marvel nor myth, nor a projection of yourself. The fruit of prayerful waiting, it comes concretely in the wake of a miracle from God.

In prayer, prayer that is always poor, like lightning rending the night, you will discover his secret: you can find fulfilment only in the presence of God . . . and also, you will awaken others to God, first and foremost, by the life you live.

With burning patience, don't worry that you can't pray well. Surely you know that any spiritual pretension is death to the soul before you begin.

Even when you cannot recognize him, will you stay close to him in long silences when nothing seems to be happening? There, with him, life's most significant decisions take shape. There the recurring "what's the use?" and the scepticism of the disillusioned melt away.

Tell him everything, and let him sing within you the radiant gift of life. Tell him everything, even what cannot be expressed and what is absurd.

When you understand so little of his language, talk to him about it.

In your struggles, he brings a few words, an intuition or an image to your mind. . . . And within you grows a desert flower, a flower of delight.

The Fire of His Forgiveness

Fulfilment? I would like to clear you a path to the springs of living water. There and nowehre else, imagination and the potent energies of risk blossom and flourish.

Don't you see? In every human being, a gift that is unique. Everything exists to a greater or lesser degree within you, every possible tendency. In you fertile fields, in you scorched deserts.

Fulfilment? Don't count yourself among those who have made it. You would lose vital energies, and the transfiguration of the will into creative potential.

No self-indulgence. Don't waste time in dead-end situations. Move on, unheasitating, to the essential step, and quickly.

Unconsciously, you may wound what you touch. Only Christ can touch without wounding.

Consider your neighbor not just in one stage of his life, but in all its phases. So don't try to separate the weeds from the wheat. You will only uproot them both and leave devastation behind you, exchanging the gleaming pearl for cracked earth that cannot hold water.

But you say, "How can I fulfil myself when there is an image from my past that covers the spring of living water in ashes?... Forget the ravages of the past? Nobody can do that; nor the still throbbing pangs of clinging regret."

But let just one sigh rise from deep within you, and already you are overflowing with confidence. What holds you in its clutches is being dealt with by God.

For you, this is prayer: "Forgive them, they don't know what they are doing; forgive me, I didn't know what I was doing."

"Love!" It's easily said. Forgiving means loving to the utmost.... Forgive not in order to change the other person but solely to follow Christ. No one can come closer to the living God than that.... And you yourself become a source of forgiveness.

In times of darkness, when life loses its meaning and you are unsure even of your own identity, a flame still burns bright enough to lighten your night ...

. . . The fire of his forgiveness plunges deep within you, dispelling your own confusion; he calls you by your name; and the fire burns away your bitterness to its very roots. That fire never says "enough."

Become What You Are

Fulfilment? Could you be hesitating over a choice for fear of making a mistake? Bogged down perhaps in the mire of indecision?

The fact is, a yes to Christ for life is surrounded by an element of error; but this is already purified, from the start, by an act of faith. So set out unseeing, taking him at his word.

Don't summon your own darkness again to cover your refusal. Happy all who tear their hand from their eyes to take the greatest of all risks, "dying and rising with Christ."

Fulfilment? Become what you are in your heart of hearts.

. . . and the gates of childhood will open, the wonder of a love.

Nov.–Dec. 1978   *Brother Roger*

Notes

Part One

1. Psalm 22:8
2. Matthew 21:31
3. Acts 3:6
4. Galatians 6:2
5. Weimarer Ausgabe, Vol. II, p. 605
6. Instructions of Pope Adrian VI to the Nuncio F. Chieregati in Karl MIRBT, *Quellen zur Geschichte des Papsttums und des romischen Katholizismus*, 5th ed., Tubingen 1934, p. 261
7. PETER THE VENERABLE, *Sermon sur la louange du Sépulcre du Seigneur*, (Revue Bénédictine) 1954, p. 242
8. SAINT BERNARD, *Letter 254*, Patrologie latine, Vol. 182, p. 461

Part Two

1. Matthew 11:12
2. Revelation 3:16
3. Ephesians 4:9
4. 1 Peter 3:19–20
5. Ephesians 3:18
6. Luke 17:10
7. 1 Corinthians 3:9
8. Mark 9:24
9. 1 Corinthians 7:20
10. Revelation 2:10
11. See Isaiah 55:10–11
12. Marc Oraison
13. Saint Ambrose, *Treatise on St. Luke's Gospel*
14. Pope John XXIII, in an address to the parish priests of Rome, 29 January 1959

15. Matthew 18:20
16. Matthew 26:26–29
17. 2 Thessalonians 1:3
18. Matthew 8:8
19. Saint John Chrysostom
20. Colossians 1:24
21. Matthew 5:9
22. Matthew 26:52
23. Pope Paul VI, Encyclical *Populorum Progressio*, 31
24. See Acts 2:42–47 and Acts 4:32–35